GAMES
M A G A Z I N E

PRESENTS

THE KIDS' GIANT BOOK OF GAMES

D1468617

GAMES MAGAZINE
PRESENTS

THE KIDS' GIANT BOOK OF GAMES

EDITED BY KAREN C. ANDERSON

TIMES
BOOKS

All rights reserved under International and Pan-American Copyright Conventions. Published in the United States by Times Books, a division of Random House, Inc., New York, and simultaneously in Canada by Random House of Canada Limited, Toronto. Most of the material in this book previously appeared in GAMES Junior magazine, which is a trademark of B. & P. Publishing Co., Inc.

ISBN: 0-8129-2199-2

Manufactured in the United States of America
9 8 7 6 5 4

Contents

PICTURE PUZZLES

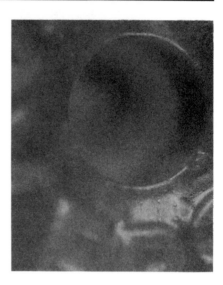

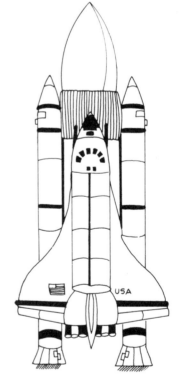

WORD PLAY

MYSTERY, LOGIC, & NUMBERS

GAMES AND TRIVIA

ANSWERS

Triangle Tangle 1

Color in each area that has exactly three sides and you'll see something that might make you open your eyes in the morning.

ANSWER, PAGE 117

ILLUSTRATION BY MARK MAZUT

Eyeball Benders 1

Can you identify the objects in these close-up photos?

ANSWERS, PAGE 117

PHOTOGRAPHS BY KEITH GLASGOW

Picture Crossword 1

To solve this crossword, enter the name of each object in its proper place in the grid.

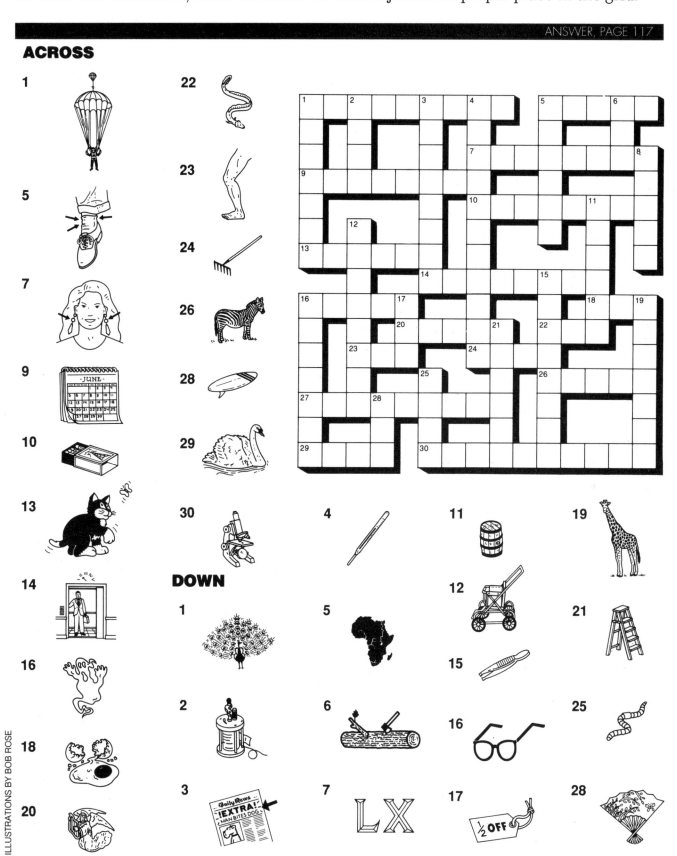

ACROSS

1
5
7
9
10
13
14
16
18
20
22
23
24
26
28
29
30

DOWN

1
2
3
4
5
6
7
11
12
15
16
17
19
21
25
28

ill-Ins

Complete each crossword grid with words that fit the given category.

ANSWERS, PAGE 117

RELATIVES

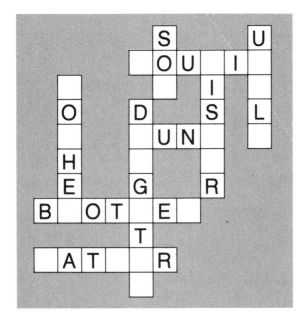

MUSICAL INSTRUMENTS

OCCUPATIONS

CLOTHING

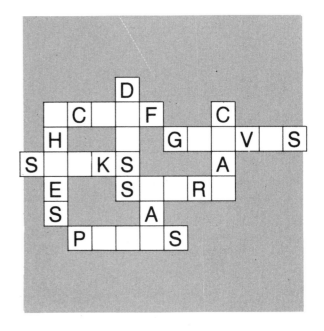

Bear Maze

Only one path will take the bear from the upper left corner of this maze to the cave at the lower right. Can you find it?

ANSWER, PAGE 117

START

FINISH

Pencil Pointers 1

In this crossword, the clues appear inside the grid. Fill in the answers in the direction of the arrows.

ANSWER, PAGE 117

Jumps on one foot ▼	Shaped like an egg ▼	Single step ▼	Flower stalk ▼	Looked unhappy	▼	Cutting tool ▼	Golf ball holder ▼	Finish ▼
►				Give a grade ►				
Big tub ►				Animals in yokes ►				
Card worth 1 point ►				Pesky plant ►				
Sour citrus fruit ►				A color ▼		Short letters ▼	Swap ▼	Logic ▼
That thing's	Melt ▼	— pop (cola) ▼	Leases ►	►				
►			Love ► / — and reel ▼					
A unicorn has one ►					Light brown ►			
Lie like __: 2 wds. ►					Boys' names ►			
Walk in the ocean ►					Look at ►			

GAMES MAGAZINE PRESENTS

Target Practice

Can you shoot five arrows into the target to score *exactly* 50 points?

ANSWER, PAGE 117

ILLUSTRATION BY JOHN O'BRIEN

Shoe Fits

Can you find at least 10 things wrong with this shoe store scene?

ANSWERS, PAGE 117

Riddle Search 1

The 20 weather words listed below are hidden in the grid of letters. Look across, back, up, down, and diagonally in the letters, and circle each word you find. The word BREEZE has been circled as an example.

When you've correctly circled all 20 words, take the uncircled letters from the grid and write them on the blank spaces at the bottom of the page. Keep the letters in order from left to right and from top to bottom, and you'll discover the answer to this riddle: THREE BIG PEOPLE WERE WALKING UNDER ONE SMALL UMBRELLA. WHY DIDN'T THEY GET WET?

ANSWER, PAGE 117

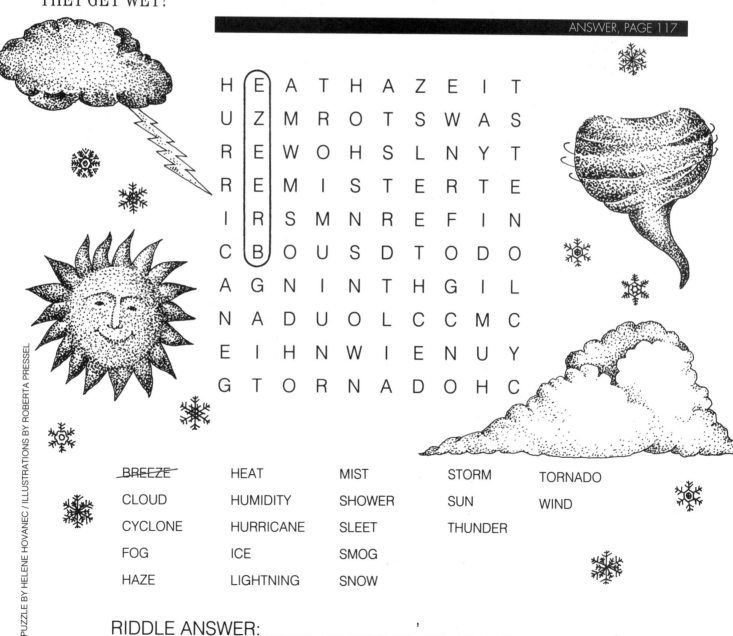

```
H E A T H A Z E I T
U Z M R O T S W A S
R E W O H S L N Y T
R E M I S T E R T E
I R S M N R E F I N
C B O U S D T O D O
A G N I N T H G I L
N A D U O L C C M C
E I H N W I E N U Y
G T O R N A D O H C
```

BREEZE · HEAT · MIST · STORM · TORNADO
CLOUD · HUMIDITY · SHOWER · SUN · WIND
CYCLONE · HURRICANE · SLEET · THUNDER
FOG · ICE · SMOG
HAZE · LIGHTNING · SNOW

RIDDLE ANSWER: __ __ __ __ __ __ __ ' __ __ __ __ __ __ __ __ __ .

Match-Up 1

These six space shuttles look similar, but only two are exactly alike. Can you find the two that match?

ANSWER, PAGE 117

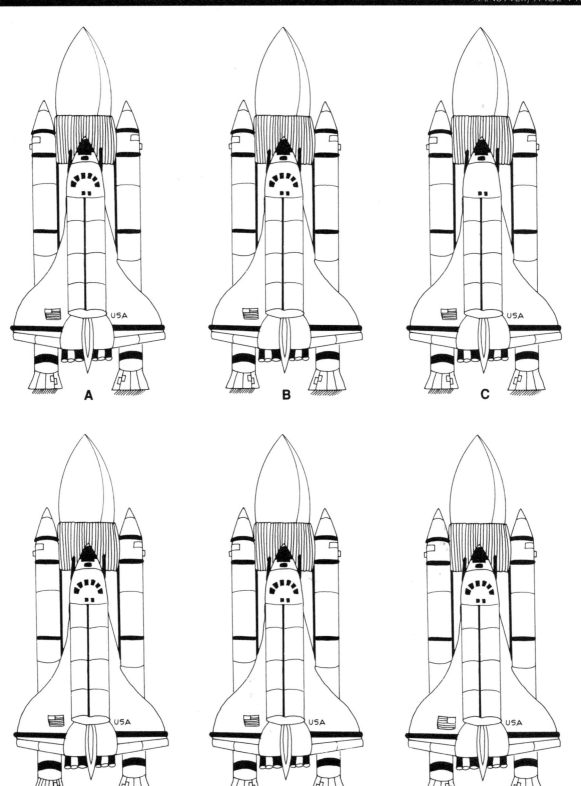

A   B   C

D   E   F

Out of Order 1

The panels of this comic strip are all mixed up. Can you unscramble the pictures so that they tell a story?

ANSWER, PAGE 117

A

B

C

D

E

F

PUZZLE AND ILLUSTRATION BY ROBERT LEIGHTON

Connect the Dots 1

Connect the dots in order from 1 to 122 to see why this chicken is in "hot water."

ANSWER, PAGE 117

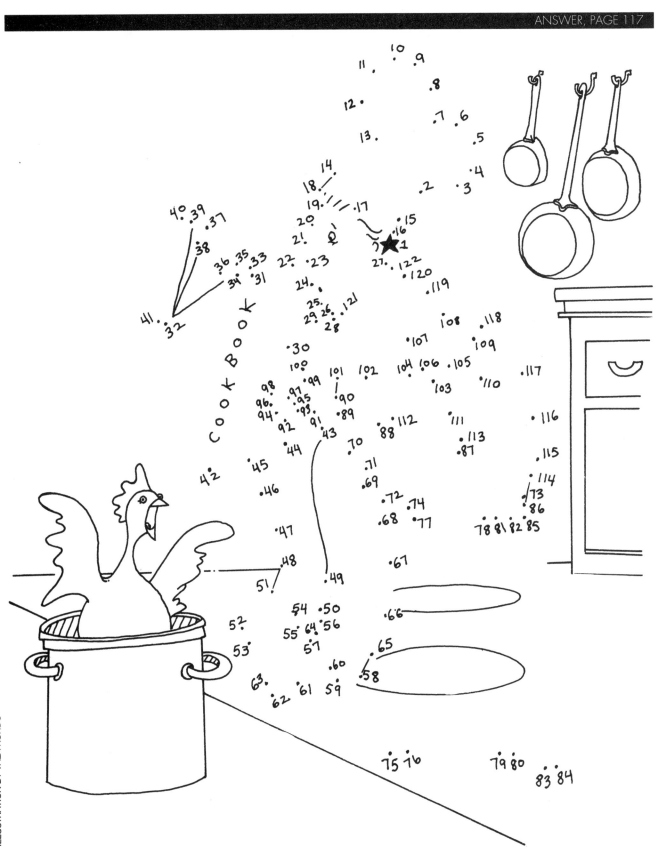

Snowed-In **P**ictures

Can you find the following things hidden in this snowy scene: banana, baseball bat, bell, boomerang, broom, candle, candy cane, comb, doughnut, fish, golf club, ice cream cone, kite, pencil, rabbit, witch hat?

ANSWERS, PAGE 118

ILLUSTRATION BY MARK MAZUT

Birthday Bash

Amy, Barbara, Cindy, Doug, and Eddy all have their birthdays today, and are seen here after opening their gifts. Barbara is the oldest and Eddy is the youngest. Amy is one year older than Eddy, but one year younger than the twins. Barbara is three years older than the second oldest in the group.

Each child has a different expression on his or her face. The ten-year-old seems content. Eddy is surprised. The youngest girl is unhappy but the second youngest girl has a broad smile. The older of the two boys, who is seven, looks confused.

Can you match the faces to the names and figure out each child's age?

ANSWERS, PAGE 118

_____   _____

_____

_____   _____

PUZZLE BY JUNO S. ROBERTS / ILLUSTRATIONS BY ROBERTA PRESSEL

Picture **A**crostic

Fill in each of the 13 words reading across with the name of one of the 15 pictures on the page, using the word lengths and given letters as guides. When all the words are filled in correctly, the shaded columns, reading down, will spell a phrase that has to do with the two unused pictures.

ANSWERS, PAGE 118

PUZZLE AND ILLUSTRATION BY ROBERT LEIGHTON

Tough Teasers

Can you figure out the surprising answers to these eight tricky questions?

ANSWERS, PAGE 118

1. If you're on a roof, holding on to a goose and a ladder, what's the quickest way to get down?

2. Sharon and Karen were born on the same day of the same year and have the same mother and father, but they are not twins. How can that be?

3. Why didn't Noah catch more fish while he was on the ark?

4. Mrs. Katz owns five gray cats, three black cats, and one white cat. How many of Mrs. Katz's cats can say that they are the same color as another of Mrs. Katz's cats?

PUZZLE BY STEPHANIE SPADACCINI / ILLUSTRATIONS BY DIANE DAWSON

6. Why are the Middle Ages called the Dark Ages?

5. Where was the *Declaration of Independence* signed?

7. The king's fool had offended him and was sentenced to death. "You have been a good fool," said the king, "therefore I will permit you to choose the manner of your death." What did the fool choose?

8. What did Washington say to his men before they got in the boat?

M Is for **M**all

In this scene, can you find 45 or more things whose names start with the letter M?

ANSWERS, PAGE 118

Picture This

To discover a picture hidden in this grid of squares, carefully color in the correct boxes in each row. In row 1, for example, color in the box in column P; and in row 2, color in the boxes in columns Q and R.

ANSWER, PAGE 119

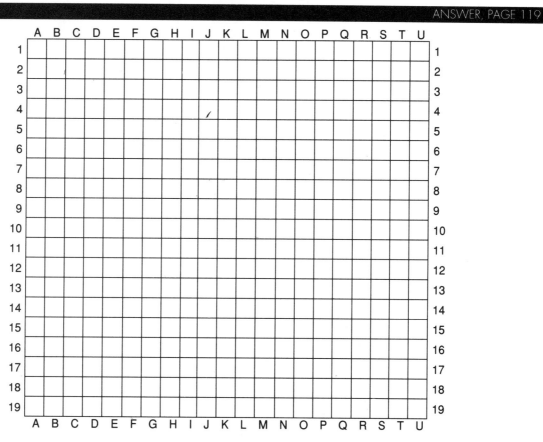

Row	1	P
Row	2	Q, R
Row	3	P, Q, R, S
Row	4	P, Q, R, S
Row	5	O, P, Q, R, S, T
Row	6	N, O, P, Q, S, T, U
Row	7	C, D, M, N, O, P, Q, T, U
Row	8	B, C, D, F, G, H, I, J, K, L, M, N, O, P, Q
Row	9	B, C, E, F, G, H, I, J, K, L, M, N, O, P
Row	10	A, B, E, F, G, H, I, J, K, L, M, N, O, P
Row	11	B, E, F, G, H, I, J, K, L, M, N, O, P, Q
Row	12	E, F, G, H, I, J, K, L, M, N, O, Q, R
Row	13	D, E, F, G, H, I, N, O, R
Row	14	D, G, H, O, Q, R
Row	15	E, G, H, O, P, Q
Row	16	E, H, O
Row	17	F, H, I, O,
Row	18	E, I, O,
Row	19	I, J, P,

Crossword 1

ANSWER, PAGE 119

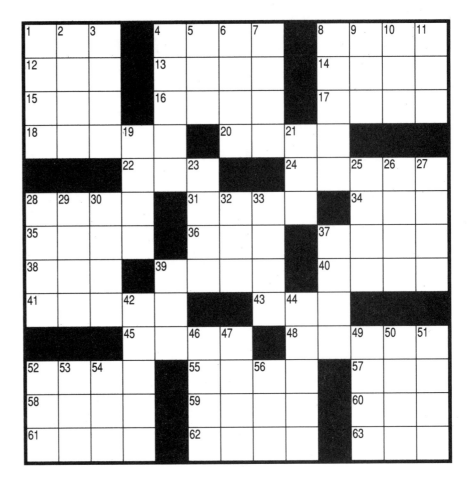

ACROSS

1 Container for cookies
4 Not that
8 The sun, for example
12 I am, you ___
13 ___ and seek
14 Love's opposite
15 Tiny
16 Not closed
17 Grew older
18 Places to keep cash or jewels
20 Eve's partner
22 Morning moisture
24 Student workplaces
28 Air pollution
31 "___ Lang Syne"
34 Bat the ball
35 Surfer's need
36 Organization that sells Thin Mint cookies: Abbreviation
37 ___ slaw
38 Ginger ___ (soft drink)
39 Ray of sunlight
40 Aid
41 One cent
43 Sheep sound
45 Snakelike water creatures
48 Large or magnificent
52 Gorillas
55 Simplicity
57 Highest card in bridge or poker
58 Loaned
59 Final word of a prayer
60 Not he or it
61 Young boys
62 Yards, divided by three
63 How many fingers you have

DOWN

1 Scary shark movie
2 What an acre measures
3 Coral barrier
4 Not these
5 Pelvis bone
6 Thought
7 Put in the mail
8 Embarrassment
9 "You're it!" game
10 Lunched
11 Rudolph's nose color
19 Rim
21 Calculate 2 + 2
23 Salary
25 Product made by Reebok
26 Exterminate
27 Staircase part
28 Trade

29 Bull's gender
30 Stove
32 Country just north of Mexico: Abbreviation
33 Baby sheep
37 Burn to a crisp
39 Opposite of "Hi!"
42 Homes for birds
44 FBI investigator
46 Tree part
47 Not different
49 Where the sun rises
50 Feel sore all over
51 High school student
52 Everyone
53 Small green vegetable
54 Finish
56 Notice or understand

PUZZLE BY ANDREA CARLA MICHAELS

Tricks and Treats

Mr. and Mrs. McMillan like to play tricks on their Halloween visitors. Before you get your Halloween treat, first you have to study their entrance hall for two minutes. Then you must turn the page and correctly answer 7 or more of the 10 questions they will ask you.

PUZZLE BY KAREN ANDERSON / ILLUSTRATION BY PHIL SCHEUER

Tricks and Treats

(PLEASE DON'T READ THIS UNTIL YOU HAVE READ THE PREVIOUS PAGE.)

ANSWERS, PAGE 119

The McMillans ask you the following questions:

1. What was the black cat playing with?
2. What was shown in the picture above the table?
3. Was the mask or the witch's hat on the right-hand side of the table?
4. Who wrote *Spook Stories*?
5. Where was the second-hand of the clock?
6. What was in the lower right-hand corner of the table?
7. What year was showing on the calendar?
8. How many spiders were there?
9. What kind of candy was in the jar?
10. Which two of these jack-o'-lanterns were on the table?

 A   B   C   D

Cross Math

Place the nine numbers below in the empty squares of the grid at right to form correct arithmetic equations in all three rows and all three columns. Each of the nine numbers must be used exactly once.

ANSWER, PAGE 119

1 2 3

3 4 6

7 8 9

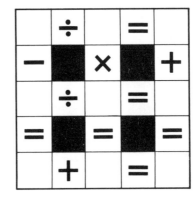

Sum Fun

To solve this rebus, first name each item shown. Then add and subtract the letters in the names, as indicated. The answer is something you can find at the movies.

ANSWER, PAGE 119

[ ][ ][ ][ ][ ] + [ ][ ][ ] + [ ][ ][ ][ ][ ]

− [ ][ ][ ][ ] + [ ][ ][ ][ ][ ][ ] + 7 + M [ ]

− [ ][ ][ ][ ][ ] − [ ][ ][ ][ ][ ][ ] = ?

[ ][ ][ ][ ][ ][ ] [ ][ ][ ][ ][ ][ ][ ][ ] [ ][ ][ ][ ][ ][ ][ ][ ]

PUZZLE BY MIKE SHENK / PHOTOGRAPHS BY KEITH GLASGOW

ConfUSAbles

Even when we see something every day, we don't always pay enough attention to remember it clearly. Test yourself on these U.S. flags, maps, and money. Put an X in the box by the choice you think is correct, and see if you can avoid getting confused.

ANSWERS, PAGE 119

1. Does the U.S. flag have 7 red stripes and 6 white stripes, or 6 red stripes and 7 white stripes?

A ☐   B ☐

2. On which map are Vermont (VT) and New Hampshire (NH) correctly labeled?

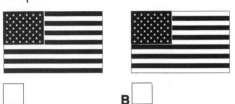

A ☐   B ☐

3. The same sections of two U. S. maps showing state outlines have been torn out. Which one is right-side up (that is, placed so that north is at the top)?

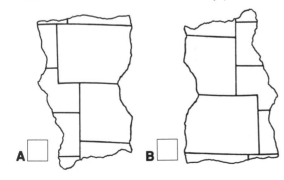

A ☐   B ☐

4. On the U.S. penny, nickel, dime, quarter, and dollar bill, which way do the presidents face? (Hint: They don't all face the same way.)

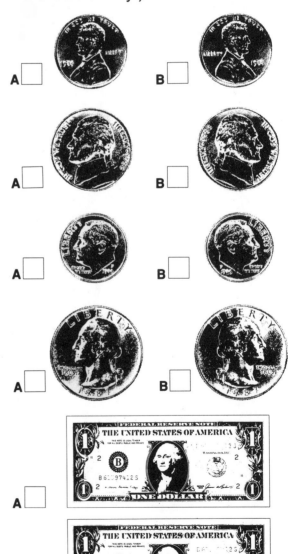

A ☐   B ☐

PUZZLE BY WAYNE SCHMITTBERGER

Money Fingers

Tell a friend or relative that your fingertips can magically feel places where money has rested. They will move a coin around this Q-shaped diagram according to a number that only they know. Without looking, you will be able to put your finger on the spot where the coin last landed.

To perform this trick, you will need to cut out or copy the diagram on this page, so that no one but you can see these directions.

Have your friend put a coin on the START circle at the bottom of the Q. Tell him or her to think of a number between 5 and 20 without telling you what it is. Turn your back, and have your friend move the coin while counting silently from 1 to the chosen number. On counting 1, your friend moves the coin to the circle just above START. On 2, the coin moves to the circle above that, and so on, with the coin moving clockwise (up and to the left) around the Q until the chosen number is reached.

Now, have your friend count the same number again, while moving the coin counterclockwise this time (starting with the circle next to the coin, retracing its path). Your back should still be turned.

Ask your friend to rub the coin on the last letter the coin landed on, to leave an invisible "mark" for your finger to detect. The coin should then be taken away. Turn back to look at the Q, and announce that you will now magically "feel" the last circle that the coin was on.

Trace the circle with your finger several times, pretending to concentrate hard. Finally, stop on the letter L, and say, "here." This will always be the letter where the coin ends up. Maybe your friend will be so amazed that you'll get to keep the coin!

Country **P**aths

Can you wind your way from the house in the upper left to the store in the lower right and avoid all the dead ends?

ANSWER, PAGE 119

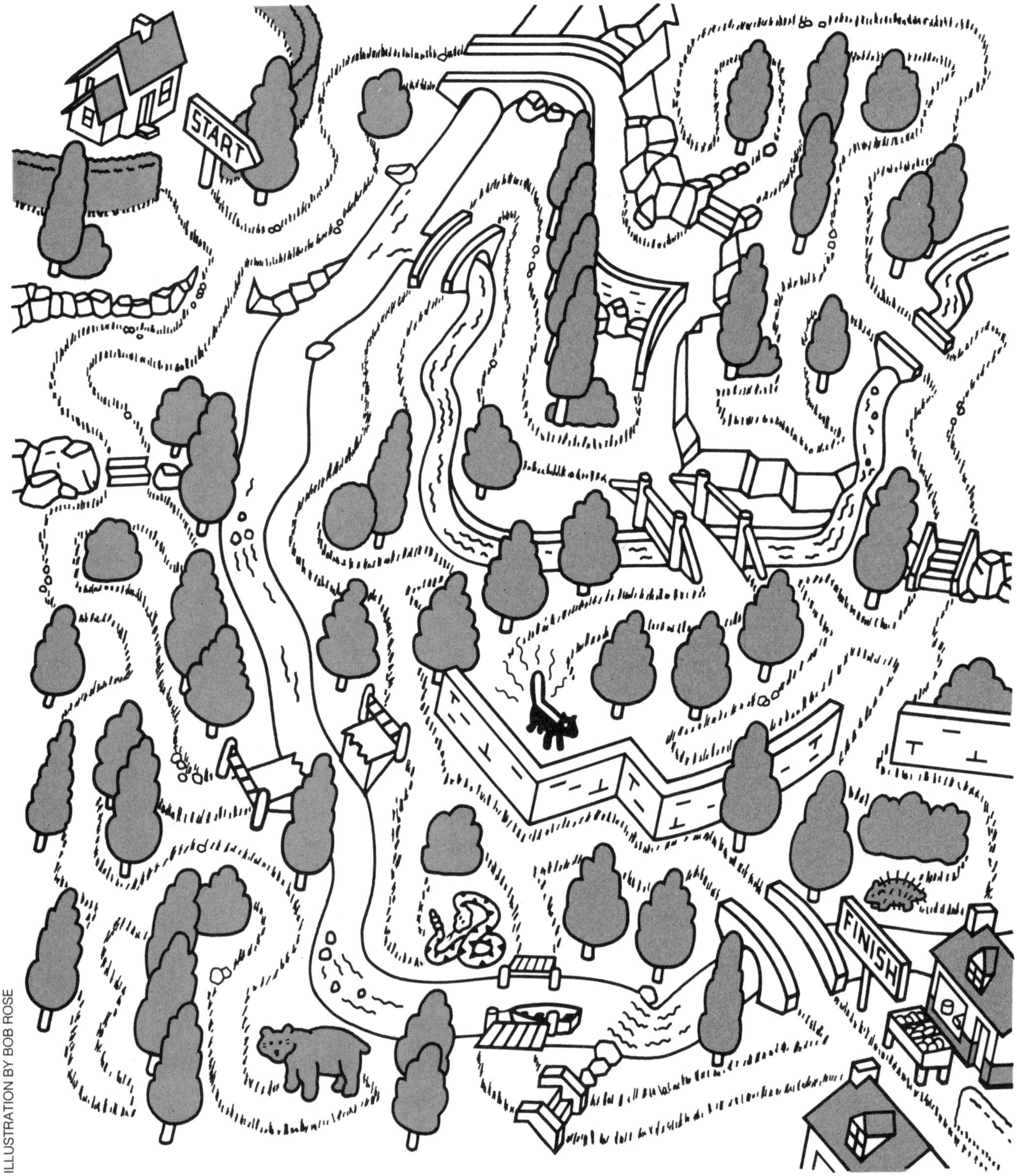

START

FINISH

Round and Round

Solving this puzzle will have you going around in circles—two of them to be exact. The clues around the outside of the circle define words to be entered as shown by the brackets. The clues on the inside define words that use the same letters as the outside words, but are split at different points. Can you fill in all the letters without getting dizzy?

ANSWER, PAGE 119

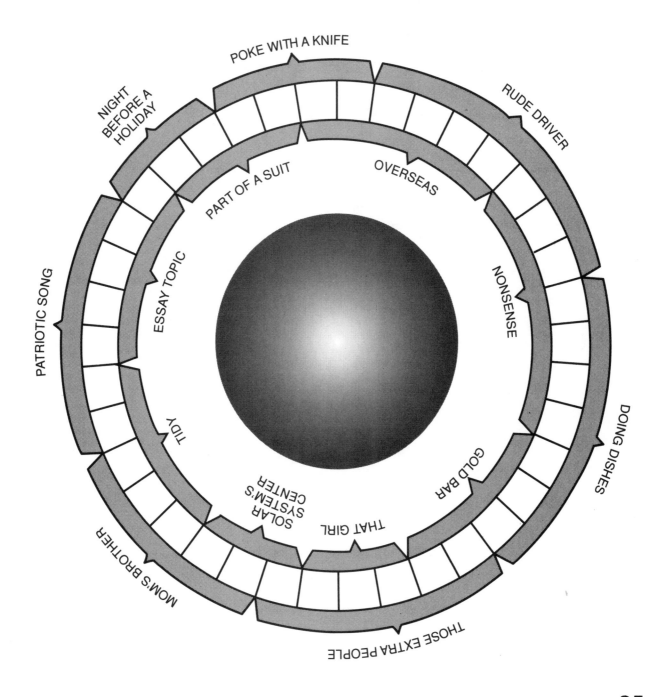

POKE WITH A KNIFE

NIGHT BEFORE A HOLIDAY

RUDE DRIVER

PART OF A SUIT

OVERSEAS

PATRIOTIC SONG

ESSAY TOPIC

NONSENSE

TIDY

DOING DISHES

MOM'S BROTHER

SOLAR SYSTEM'S CENTER

THAT GIRL

GOLD BAR

THOSE EXTRA PEOPLE

PUZZLE BY GEORGE BREDEHORN

Lost in Space

Can you find the following things hidden in this outer space scene: banana, baseball bat, bell, bunch of carrots, coat hanger, cup, doughnut, eyeglasses, hot dog, light bulb, man in the moon, pencil, safety pin, sailboat, silhouette of a face, swan, tennis racket, wishbone?

ANSWERS, PAGE 119

ILLUSTRATION BY MARK MAZUT

Crisscross 1

Place the colorful words below into the diagram so that they interlock as in a crossword. When you are done, each word will have been used exactly once. One word has been filled in to start you off. (Note: Ignore the spaces in IRON GRAY and SEA GREEN, and write them in as though they were single words.)

ANSWER, PAGE 120

3 LETTERS	PLUM	IVORY	ORANGE	SCARLET
RED	ROSE	PEACH	RUSSET	
TAN		PEARL	SILVER	**8 LETTERS**
	5 LETTERS	SEPIA	VIOLET	CARDINAL
4 LETTERS	AMBER			IRON GRAY
BLUE	CORAL	**6 LETTERS**	**7 LETTERS**	LAVENDER
NAVY	EBONY	AUBURN	CRIMSON	SAPPHIRE
	HAZEL	MAROON	MAGENTA	SEA GREEN

Playing Cards

Can you spot 15 or more mistakes in this card store scene?

ANSWERS, PAGE 120

Crossword 2

ACROSS

1 Drill part
4 Ugly rodent
7 No ifs, ___, or buts
11 High card in poker
12 The last three sounds in "Old MacDonald Had a Farm"
13 Jewish book of scripture
15 Insect that might sting Bambi
17 Like very old bread
18 Nose-blowing paper
20 Diamond or ruby
21 Clothing tag
24 Mexican sandwich or salad
26 Ostrich-like bird
27 Where the moon rises
30 One-twelfth of a foot
33 New Jersey basketball team
35 Fib
36 Bushy hairstyle
37 Against: Prefix
38 Months when baseball season starts: Abbreviation
40 Once around the track
41 School test
43 Herb which is a homophone of TIME
45 Make a mistake
47 Yogi Bear's sidekick
50 Cartoon duck
52 Lightning bug
56 Farm buildings
57 President Eisenhower's nickname
58 Salmon eggs
59 Colors T-shirts
60 Koppel of ABC News
61 "___ a beautiful day in the neighborhood"

DOWN

1 Opposite of good
2 Cubes in the freezer
3 Golfer's prop
4 Do one's nails again
5 Is sick
6 Playthings
7 Out on a boat: 2 words
8 "To be or ___ to be"
9 Long-winged mosquito-eating insect
10 Flea market event
14 Shorten pants
16 Rural ___: Abbreviation
19 Say
21 Singer Horne
22 Prayer's ending
23 Colorful former caterpillar
25 U.S. spy organization: Abbreviation
28 Site of 1836 battle for Texas independence
29 Drink through a straw
31 Stuff (full)
32 Comedian Bob
34 Number of players on a volleyball team
39 Stashed food
42 Deep chasm
44 Gardening tool
45 Asner and Mister
46 Bug spray brand
48 Just for the fun ___: 2 words
49 Ten-speed or tandem
51 Enemy
53 Last day of the school week: Abbreviation
54 Parking area
55 Word of agreement

PUZZLE BY KAREN ANDERSON

Detective's Notebook 1

FILE: CRIME SOLVING
CATEGORY: PICTURE MYSTERY

When Officer Fred Dumpty entered Bell's Hobby Shop, Mr. Bell was leaning against the counter, head in hands, as if he were in pain.

Looking up, he said in a voice that cracked, "Nancy Gibson. She must have stolen the Silver Arrow. And to think I trusted her."

The Silver Arrow was the most expensive model locomotive in the store, a collector's item that worked better than some real-life Amtrak engines.

Mr. Bell pointed to the display shelf, where a line of passenger cars sat on the tracks. The engine was missing.

Dumpty scratched his head and took out his notepad, musing to himself, "How come the Sergeant sends Mallory to investigate bank robberies and I get stolen choo-choo trains?" But then he thought, "No case was too small for a great detective like Sherlock Holmes to solve, and no case is too small for Officer Dumpty!" Speaking aloud, Dumpty said, "What makes you think it was the Gibson girl?"

The owner hesitated, as if he didn't really want to get Nancy in trouble. "Nancy loves collecting things—toy soldiers, thimbles, wind-up toys. And especially model trains. She always stops here after school and plays with the Silver Arrow. She wanted to buy it, but she said it would take a long time to save up for it on her allowance."

"When do you think it was stolen?" Dumpty asked Mr. Bell.

"It couldn't have been more than a half hour ago," Mr. Bell replied. "Around 8:30. I was closing my store for the night and went into the back room. When I returned, the train was gone. That's when I phoned the police."

It was a long, hot drive to the Gibson home. Dumpty rolled down the window to cool off. To save gas money, the Sarge told his men to turn off their air conditioning. Well, Sherlock Holmes didn't have air conditioning in 221B Baker Street, either. When a sweaty Dumpty arrived, he rang the bell several times. No one answered. Dumpty decided to wait.

After 15 minutes, Officer Dumpty knocked as loudly as he could. A

minute or two later, Nancy Gibson opened the door.

"Where have you been?" Dumpty asked sharply. The heat was making him irritable.

"I was reading *Antique Model Railroad* magazine in my clubhouse in the backyard. I built the clubhouse to keep all the things I collect. It's much cooler in there. With the door open, there's a nice breeze."

Officer Dumpty gave the girl his sternest look, one he had practiced in front of the mirror. "Someone stole the Silver Arrow from Bell's. Do you know anything about it?"

Nancy Gibson stared at him, eyes wide with innocence. "Gee, officer, it wasn't me. Take a look at my clubhouse—I'll even let you in without a search warrant."

They walked to the backyard and opened the clubhouse door. The room was pitch black. Nancy lit the candle on the table.

"If you were reading in here," said Dumpty, "how come the candle is out?" Gotcha, thought the officer.

Said Nancy coolly, "I blew it out when I went to see who was

WRITTEN BY MARVIN MILLER / ILLUSTRATION BY PHIL SCHEUER

knocking."

Darn, thought Dumpty, she's quick. The officer scanned the room, filled with thimbles and toys and wind-up toys and model railroad trains. But no Silver Arrow. Nancy shrugged her shoulders.

Sherlock would never have been outwitted by a 13-year-old, thought Dumpty, desperately. He looked at the room again and this time he had an idea. He turned to Nancy:

"You're sure you were here tonight?" She nodded with a smile.

"Well," said Dumpty, "I know for a fact you weren't in your clubhouse when I rang your doorbell. At that moment, I suspect you were still returning from Bell's Hobby Shop, and I'll bet you had the Silver Arrow with you. You must have used the back door so that I wouldn't see you arrive."

"How do you know that?" asked Nancy.

"Elementary," replied the officer.

AT LEFT IS A PICTURE OF OFFICER DUMPTY SPEAKING WITH NANCY GIBSON. WHY DID HE THINK SHE WAS LYING?

FILE: DETECTIVE TIPS
CATEGORY: TOP SECRET

Using a water glass, you can overhear a suspect's conversation in the next room. Hold the glass tightly against the wall and put your ear to its open end. The larger the glass and the thinner its sides, the better you will be able to hear.

FILE: MISCELLANEOUS
CATEGORY: MYSTERY RIDDLE

Two policemen hid behind a hedge to watch for speeders they could give tickets to. One policeman looked up the road, the other looked down it, so as to cover both directions.

"Bill," said one, without turning his head, "what are you smiling at?"
HOW COULD HE TELL THAT BILL WAS SMILING?

FILE: CRIME CLUES
CATEGORY: SPOTTING SPOTS

Detectives can discover clues by studying spots. Below are different drop marks left by a person eating a chocolate ice cream cone. The marks were made by the dripping ice cream.

Can you match the drops (1-6) with the descriptions of the person eating the cone (A-F)?

A—standing on the ground
B—sitting on top of a ladder
C—standing in the same place for several minutes
D—walking toward your right
E—walking toward your left
F—standing on a balcony above a wall

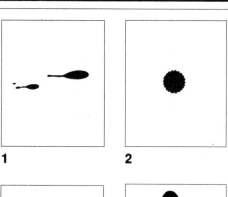

1 **2** **3**

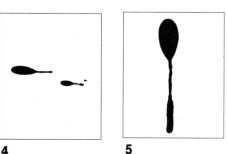

4 **5** **6**

Indian Maze

Can you help the Indian find the way back to his teepee?

ANSWER, PAGE 120

Santa Says . . .

Santa Claus has sent you a hidden message. To find it, carefully shade in all of these letters wherever they appear: B, C, G, S, T, U, X, Z.

ANSWER, PAGE 120

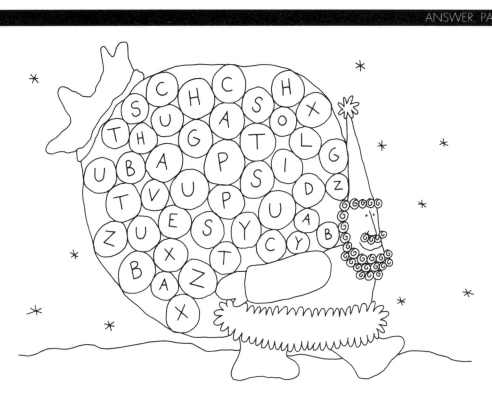

PUZZLE AND ILLUSTRATION BY DAVID LAROCHELLE

Unrhymes

Words that have the same endings often rhyme (like THUMB and DUMB), but sometimes they do not (like BEAD and DEAD). Can you complete each list of words in such a way that none of the words in any list rhyme with each other? Place one letter on each blank space.

ANSWERS, PAGE 120

PUZZLE BY GEORGE BREDEHORN

1. H O U R
    _ O U R
    _ O U R

2. T O E S
    _ O E S
    _ _ O E S

3. S O U L
    _ O U L
    _ _ O U L

4. M A I D
    _ A I D
    _ _ A I D

Undersea Hunt

Can you find the following things hidden in this underwater scene: arrow, banana, bird, book, boomerang, crocodile, eyeglasses, funnel, key, pizza slice, ruler, scissors, snake, spoon, watermelon slice?

ANSWERS, PAGE 120

PUZZLE AND ILLUSTRATION BY MARK MAZUT

Making Connections

This is a game for two or more players. Each player in turn draws a straight line between any two consecutive letters of the alphabet. For example, a player could connect A to B, C to D, or L to M. A line may never cross a line that has already been drawn. The last player to draw a permissible line wins. In game #2, the rules are the same, except that players connect consecutive numbers instead of letters.

GAME 1

N C O E F S R Q P X G Z M L D W B Y T J A I U K V H

GAME 2

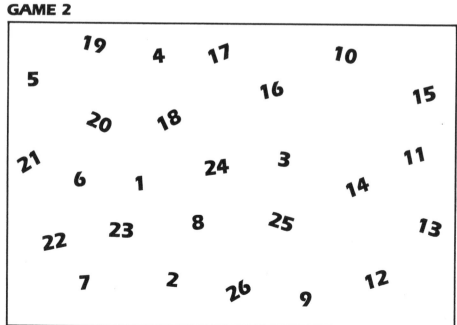

Picture Crossword 2

To solve this crossword, enter the name of each object in its proper place in the grid.

ANSWER, PAGE 120

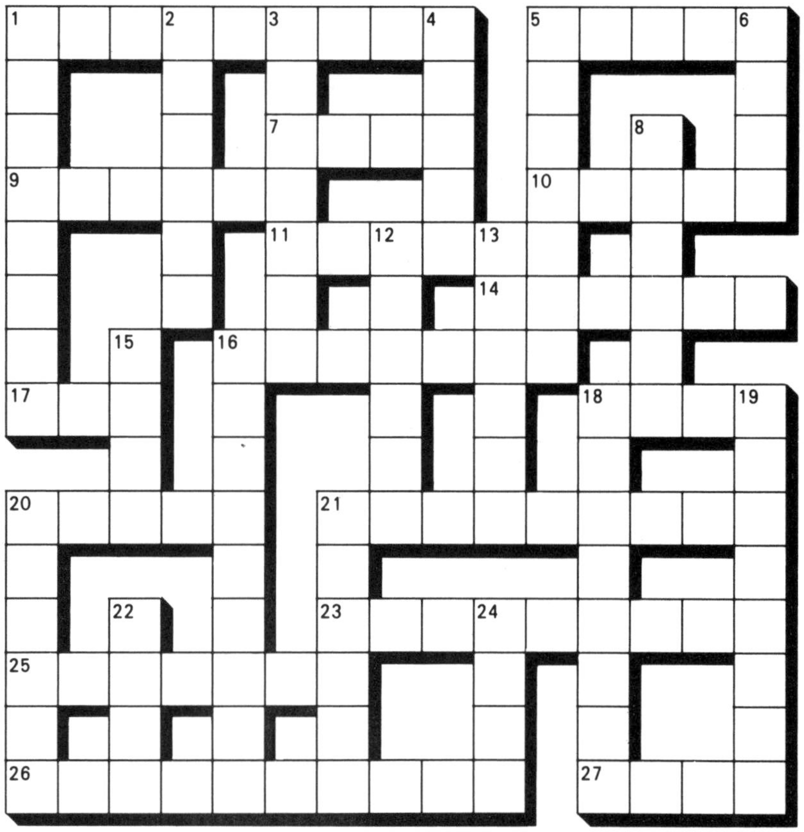

ACROSS

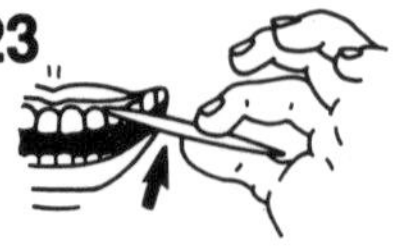

1 
21
5 
23
7 
25
9 
26
10 
27
11

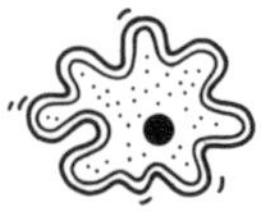

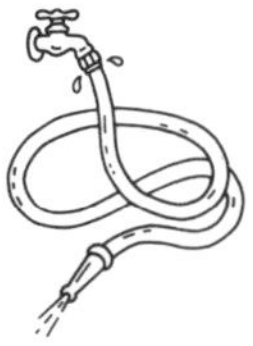

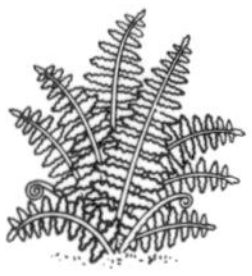

DOWN

14 
1
16 
2
17 
18
3
20

4
8
16
20
12
18
21 
13
22 
5
15
19
24
6

Computer ating

These three computers have each been programmed to give advice for a computer dating service. Unfortunately, errors were made in programming two of the computers. One of them gives advice that is always incorrect. Another always alternates correct and incorrect statements. The remaining computer makes only correct statements.

Julie is considering dating either Bob, Charles, or Arthur. She has asked the three computers which of the three boys she should date, and their responses are shown on the screens.

Should Julie date Bob, Charles, or Arthur?

1

DATE BOB.

COMPUTER #3 ALWAYS TELLS THE TRUTH!

2

DATE ARTHUR.
DON'T DATE BOB.

3

DON'T DATE BOB.
DON'T DATE ARTHUR.
COMPUTER #1 ALWAYS LIES!

PUZZLE BY GEORGE BREDEHORN / ILLUSTRATION BY TOM CUSHWA

Out of **O**rder **2**

The panels of this comic strip are all mixed up. Can you unscramble the pictures so that they tell a story?

ANSWER, PAGE 121

A

B

C

D

E

F

PUZZLE AND ILLUSTRATION BY ROBERT LEIGHTON

From **S**tart to **F**inish

Can you match the raw materials (1–6) with the final products (A–F) which can be made from them?

ANSWERS, PAGE 121

Party Mix

These pictures were taken at a recent birthday party, but they have gotten mixed up. By looking at the photos carefully, and using a little logic, can you figure out the order in which they were taken?

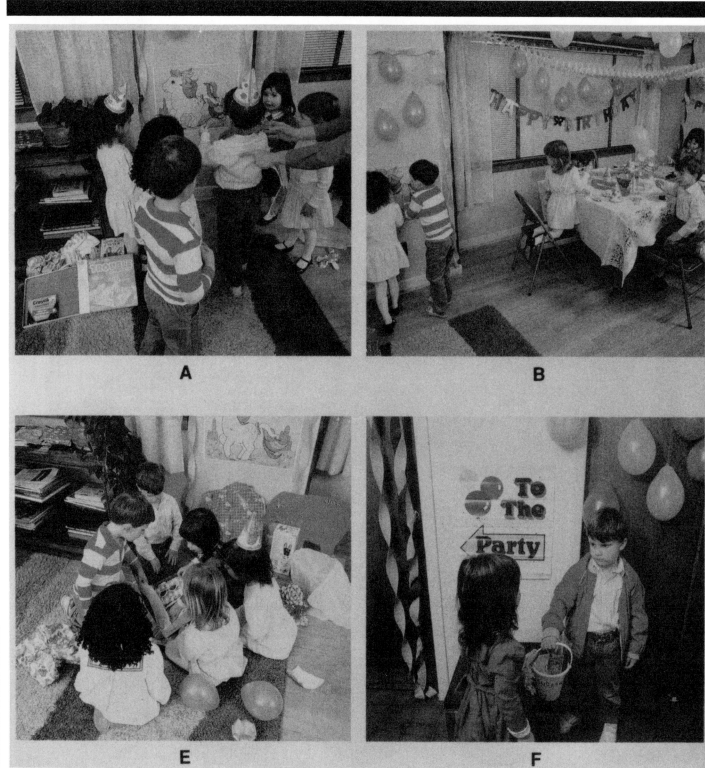

A

B

E

F

PHOTOGRAPHS BY KEITH GLASGOW

C

D

G

H

Riddle Search 2

Hidden among the letters of the grid below are the names of 26 playthings. To find them in the grid, look across, back, down, up, and diagonally. Circle each one you find. The word BALLOON has been circled as an example.

When you've circled all 26 words, take the uncircled letters from the grid and write them on the blank spaces at the bottom of the page. Keep the letters in order, from left to right and from top to bottom, and you'll discover the answer to this riddle:

WHY WAS JUNIOR WEARING A SAFARI HAT AND CARRYING A LARGE BOX WITH HUGE, STUFFED DICE?

ANSWERS, PAGE 121

```
B  S  K  A  T  E  B  O  A  R  D
C  I  Y  E  M  A  G  N  I  W  S
R  G  B  A  L  G  E  C  I  D  E
A  A  L  L  B  M  M  R  P  K
Y  E  O  H  O  C  A  A  O  U  I
O  O  C  O  A  G  C  R  N  D  B
N  P  K  R  N  H  P  B  O  A  T
O  E  S  E  E  M  T  L  I  R  R
G  T  T  S  U  N  L  E  P  T  U
A  G  S  J  A  C  K  S  O  S  C
W  H  I  S  T  L  E  E  T  I  K
```

BALLOON	CHESS	GAME	PET
BIKE	CLAY	JACKS	SKATEBOARD
BLOCKS	CRAYON	JUMPROPE	SWING
BOAT	DARTS	KITE	TOP
BOOK	DICE	MAGNET	TRUCK
CARDS	DOLL	MARBLES	WAGON
CARS			WHISTLE

ANSWER: He was going _ _ _   _ _ _ _ _   _ _ _ _ _ _ _.

Snowbawling

Your big brother has just played a trick on your little brother. You saw the whole thing (that's you in the window). Study the scene for up to two minutes, turn the page, and be ready to prove that he's guilty.

PUZZLE BY KAREN ANDERSON / ILLUSTRATION BY PHIL SCHEUER

Snowbawling

(PLEASE DON'T READ THIS UNTIL YOU HAVE READ THE PREVIOUS PAGE.)

ANSWERS, PAGE 121

1. What did your big brother do to Junior?
2. What did the snowman have on his head?
3. Are the decorations off the tree yet?
4. What pattern was on the scarf that big brother wore?
5. Was the mailbox flag up or down?
6. How many mittens was the snowman wearing?
7. Was an airplane in the sky?
8. How many hats were in the whole scene?
Bonus Question: What was the name of the street?

Match-**U**p **2**

These six sprites look similar, but only two are exactly alike. Can you find the two that match?

ANSWER, PAGE 121

A B C

D E F

PUZZLE AND ILLUSTRATION BY TED ENIK

Word Bingo

In this Bingo game, we've given you all the pieces you need to win. Your challenge is to find out which row, column, or corner-to-corner diagonal is the winner.

Pick a word on the Bingo chart. Then look for a disc that has a homophone of that word (one that sounds the same but is spelled differently, like HOUR for OUR). If you find a homophone, write it in the chart. Try to fill in a straight line of five homophones. There's only one line that wins. Can you find it?

ANSWER, PAGE 121

B	I	N	G	O
SOME ____	WASTE ____	FLOUR ____	SEW ____	ONE ____
CORPS ____	SCENTS ____	HAIR ____	EIGHT ____	TWO ____
TOE ____	PAIL ____	FREE	WHOLE ____	REEL ____
PEAR ____	GUESSED ____	DYE ____	BLUE ____	THROUGH ____
POOR ____	SALE ____	WRITE ____	VEIN ____	GNU ____

Discs: BLEW, TOW, PALE, THREW, DIE, LED, CORE, SAIL, HOLE, FLOWER, WAIST, WON, HARE, TO, SEA, SUM, CHEWS, HERE, SLAY, VAIN, GUEST, KNIGHT, CENTS, POUR

A **M**agic **S**pell

Using this card trick, you can appear to take a stack of cards arranged by a friend and magically give them an uncanny order.

To do this trick, you need two decks of cards with identical backs. Before your friend arrives, remove the 13 spades from one deck and arrange them as shown above.

The cards should be stacked so that if they are placed face down on the table, the 3 is on the top of the stack and the 5 is on the bottom.

Hide these 13 cards—either in your lap (if you are sitting at a table) or behind your back (tucked into your belt, perhaps). The rest of the first deck is not used in this trick, and should be put out of sight.

When your friend arrives, have him or her take the other deck of cards and remove all of the spades. Then ask your friend to shuffle the spades any number of times, and hand them to you.

After taking the spades from your friend, place them under the table or behind your back (whichever place you hid your prearranged set of cards). Using all your acting skills, say some magic words (make up anything you like), and pretend that you are rearranging the cards, without looking at them, until they "feel" right.

While you are pretending to rearrange the cards, exchange them with the 13 spades you set up beforehand. Bring these presorted cards in front of you, keeping them face down in a stack. Now you are ready to perform the following amazing feat.

Spell the names of each card aloud, starting with A-C-E. Each time you say a letter, move a card from the top of the pile to the bottom, keeping it face down. For example, as you begin by spelling A-C-E, move a total of three cards, on at a time, to the bottom of the pile.

When you finish spelling a card, pause, and turn the next card in the pile face up—in this case, the card you turn up will be the ace you just spelled! Remove the ace from the deck, then continue by spelling T-W-O. As before, move one card to the bottom for each letter, then turn over and remove the next card—which will be the 2.

Continue in the same way, spelling and removing the cards in order (3, 4, etc.). The last card you have left will be the king. We think your friend will be very impressed.

WRITTEN BY LOUIS PHILLIPS

B Is for **B**icycling

In this scene, can you find 50 or more things whose names start with the letter B?

ANSWERS, PAGE 121

ILLUSTRATION BY TED ENIK

Shady Shapes

To complete this picture, you must use a pencil to shade some of the white squares in one of these five patterns: ◪ ◩ ⬔ ⬕ ■. The instructions below will tell you which squares should be shaded in which pattern. For example, since "H2" is listed with the first pattern, you should find the square that is located where column H crosses row 2, and then color it to match the first pattern (◪).

ANSWER, PAGE 121

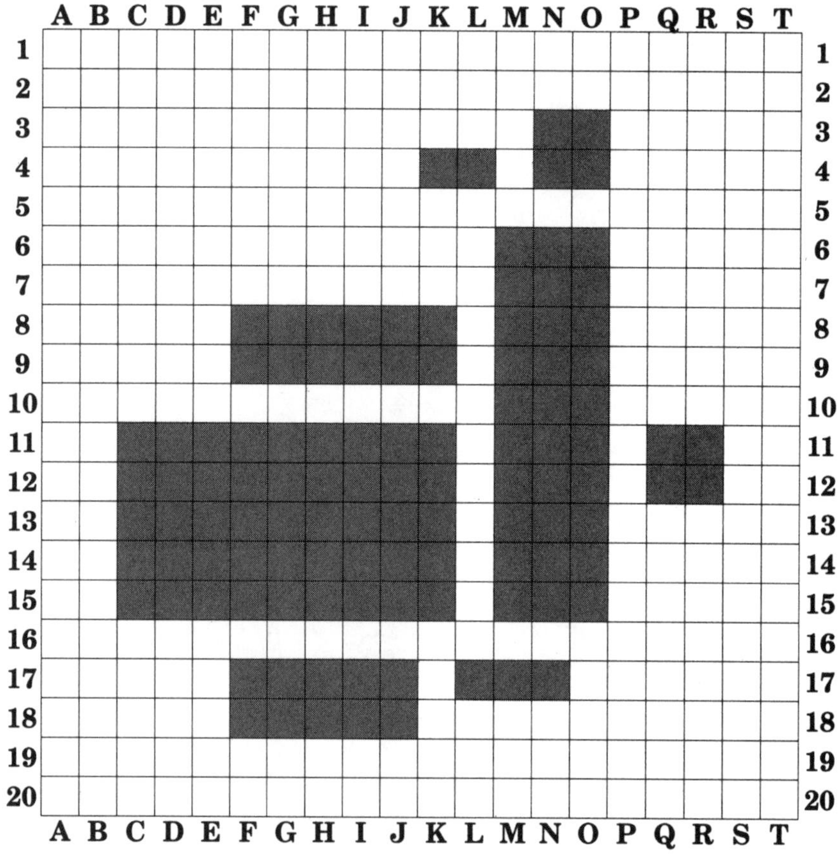

Use this pattern ◪ to shade these squares: H2 E8 D9 C10 B14

Use this pattern ◩ to shade these squares: S13 P15 O16

Use this pattern ⬔ to shade these squares: I3 J4 K5 L7 B17 E18

Use this pattern ⬕ to shade these squares: N1 K2 O2 L3 M4 Q8 R9 P10 S11 K18 Q17

Use this pattern ■ to shade these squares:

I2 J2 N2 J3 K3 L5 M5 N5 O5 L6 P8 E9 L9 P9 Q9 D10 E10 F10 G10 H10 I10 J10 K10 L10 Q10 R10 L11 P11 L12 P12 S12 L13 P13 Q13 R13 L14 P14 B15 L15 B16 C16 D16 E16 F16 G16 H16 I16 J16 K16 L16 M16 N16 C17 D17 E17 K17 O17 P17

PUZZLE BY MARK MAZUT

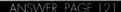

Picture Crossword 3

To solve this crossword, enter the name of each object in its proper place in the grid.

ANSWER, PAGE 121

ACROSS

1.
5.
9.
11.
12.
13.
14.
16.
20.
21.
22.
24.
26.
28.
31.
33.
34.
35.

DOWN

1.
2.
3.
4.
6.
7.
8.
10.
15.
17.
18.
19.
23.
24.
25.
27.
28.
29.
30.
32.

Eyeball Benders 2

What are these objects? And where can they all be found?

ANSWERS, PAGE 121

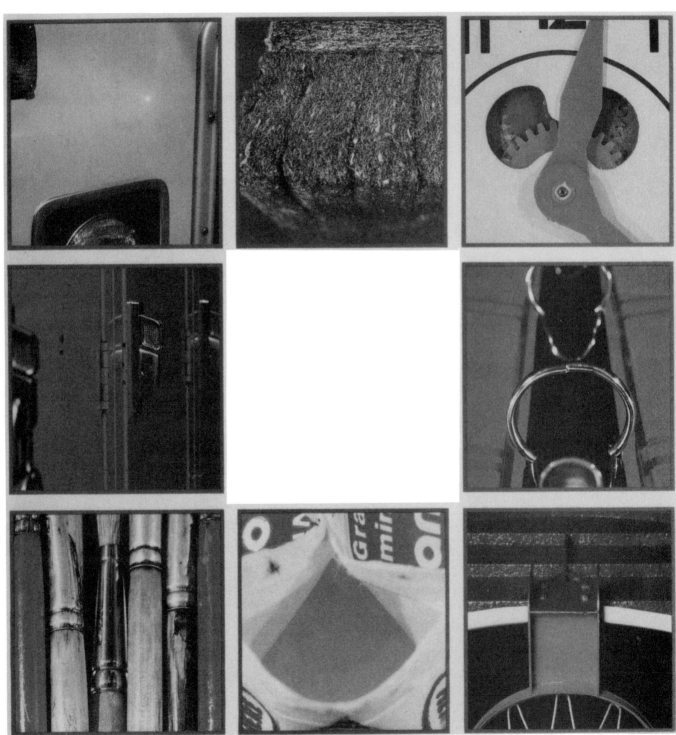

GAMES MAGAZINE PRESENTS

Squared Away

To complete this puzzle, place the words in the grids to make two 4 x 4 crosswords in which all 16 of the words appear. Two of the words have been given to start you off.

ANSWERS, PAGE 121

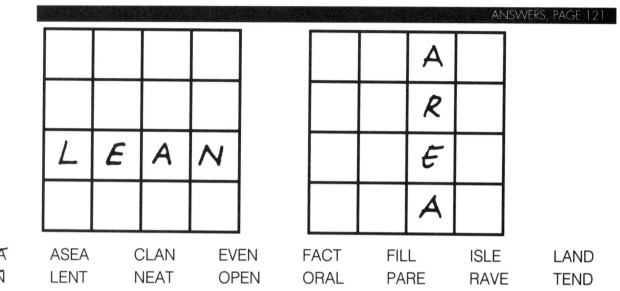

| AREA | ASEA | CLAN | EVEN | FACT | FILL | ISLE | LAND |
| LEAN | LENT | NEAT | OPEN | ORAL | PARE | RAVE | TEND |

Build a Word

Listed below are two sets of three-letter words. Each word in column A can be combined with some word in column B, with the column A word coming first, to form a new word. But be careful: One beginning may match more than one ending, but only one combination will use every word. We've done one to get you started.

ANSWERS, PAGE 121

A	B	
rat	age	_ration_
per	bid	_____
man	did	_____
kit	her	_____
for	ion	_____
fat	key	_____
don	pet	_____
car	son	_____
can	ten	_____
but	ton	_____

PUZZLE BY O.J. ROBERTSON

PUZZLE BY KAREN ANDERSON

Out of Order 3

The panels of this comic strip are all mixed up. Can you unscramble the pictures so that they tell a story?

ANSWER, PAGE 121

A

B

C

D

E

F

PUZZLE AND ILLUSTRATION BY ROBERT LEIGHTON

Connect the **D**ots **2**

Connect the dots in order from 1 to 70 to find out one way to keep cool in the summer.

ILLUSTRATION BY MARK MAZUT

Crisscross 2

Place the names of the body parts below into the diagram so that they interlock as in a crossword. When you are done, each word will have been used exactly once. One word has been filled in to start you off.

ANSWER, PAGE 122

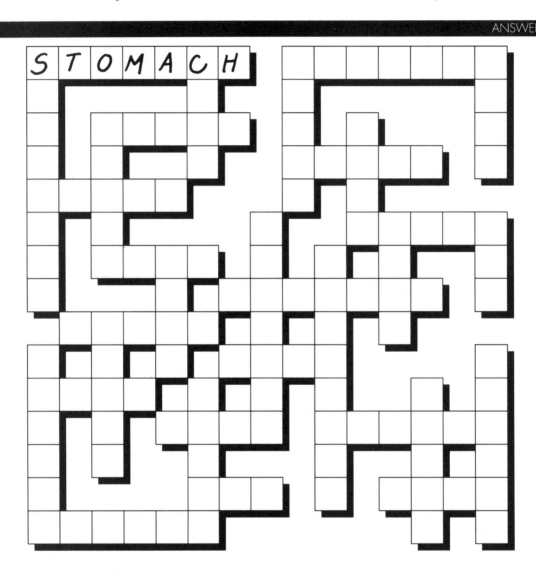

3 LETTERS
HIP
LEG

4 LETTERS
BONE
CALF

FACE
FOOT
HEAD
HEEL
KNEE
LUNG
NOSE

SHIN

5 LETTERS
ANKLE
CHEST
ELBOW
HEART

LIVER
MOUTH
NAILS
NAVEL
THIGH
TOOTH

6 LETTERS
EYELID
KIDNEY
THROAT
TONGUE

7 LETTERS
ABDOMEN

MUSCLES
RIB CAGE
~~STOMACH~~

8 LETTERS
FOREHEAD
SHOULDER

Dragon Maze

Can you help the lost knight find his way back to the castle? He is not afraid to go near the dragon, but he must stay on the paths.

ANSWER, PAGE 122

FINISH

START

ILLUSTRATION BY ROBERTA COLLIER

Skin Swap

Each of the four animals in the left-hand column has traded its fur, feathers, or scales with one of the animals on the right. Can you figure out which pairs of animals should swap skins to be normal again?

ANSWERS, PAGE 122

Pencil Pointers 2

In this crossword, the clues appear inside the grid. Fill in the answers in the direction of the arrows.

Peach's center	Pesky kid	Foot part	Pose a question	▼	— of Troy	Contact lens's place	Oceans	▼	In the past	Number of fingers
▶	▼	▼	Not he ▶ / Pounded down			▼	Have a meal	▶	▼	▼
Popular zoo animal	▶		▼				How old you are / Shop	▶		
Split __ soup	▶		Teacher's study plan	▶			▼			
Healthy	Go out, like the tide	Frost Civil War general ▶			Hallow-een's month		Sticky tree stuff	The first woman	Perceive
▶	▼	▼	Lassos	▶	▼		▼	▼	▼
Honey maker	▶		Guide a ship	Really want	▶				
Flower gardens	▶		▼	Wigwam					
Rasp	Music from Tone-Loc	High card, often	A pair ▶ / __ la la			Metal-filled rock	Hotel	Tell a fib	Stitch
▶	▼	▼	▼	Makes hot water	▶	▼	▼	▼	▼
Unit of land	▶			Bert's Muppet friend	▶				
Certain fruit	▶			Keep a magazine coming	▶				

PUZZLE BY TRIP PAYNE

Science **T**easers

Science is not just a subject you study in school. Everything we see or do in our daily lives is based in some way on science. Ten of these everyday things are described below—but they're not all described correctly! Read each description, think about it, and decide whether it's true or false. Then check your answers with the correct ones. If you like, try some of the experiments yourself. You may want to ask an adult or older family member for help.

1. If you hold a thermometer in your hand, you can make the temperature reading go up just by thinking about heat.

2. When you crack a whip, it makes a loud snapping noise because the end of the whip turns back and hits itself. The reason a whip sometimes doesn't snap is because sometimes it fails to hit itself.

3. Place two empty soda cans next to each other on their sides, separated by a few inches. If you blow hard between them, they will roll toward each other. Blowing reduces the air pressure between cans, allowing the pressure from the sides to push them together.

4. A piece of ice will float in the middle of a bowl of warm water, but it will move toward the edge of a bowl of cold water. The reason is that the warm water causes the ice to melt faster in all directions, which keeps it in the middle.

5. If you fill a glass with water that has been dyed with food coloring, and then add bleach, the water will become clear.

WRITTEN BY KAREN ANDERSON / ILLUSTRATIONS BY KIM WILSON EVERSZ

6. You can pour air just as if it were liquid. Collect cold air in a closed box by putting the box in your freezer. If you then hold the box high over your head, remove the lid, and turn the box over, you will actually feel the cold air coming down. That's because the cold air is heavier than the warmer air in the room.

7. It's easy to spin an egg on a plate, but only when it's a hard-boiled egg. If you try to spin an uncooked egg, it stops very quickly. The reason is that the yolk inside is so loose (cooking makes it hard) that it prevents the egg from keeping its balance.

8. Normally, water will run through a fine-meshed strainer, However, if you first dip the strainer in cooking oil, the oil will form a lining and the strainer will hold a great deal of water.

9. When a slice of bread with peanut butter on one side falls off a table, it will always land with the peanut butter side down. That's the heavier side, so no matter which way it starts to fall, the heavier side will end up on the bottom.

10. If the lid of a jar is lined with rubber, heating the lid to get it open won't work. The reason is that heat makes the rubber expand, which only makes the lid tighter.

Alphabet **S**tew

Fill the blank columns with the 26 letters of the alphabet so that a seven-letter word is spelled in every row. You may cross off each letter of the alphabet as you use it, because it will be used only once. As an example, the letter C has been filled in the first row to complete the word POPCORN.

ANSWERS, PAGE 122

A B ~~C~~ D E F G H I J K L M N O P Q R S T U V W X Y Z

P O P C O R N   B A R __ E L L

C H O __ D E R   C O N __ U R E

D I S __ A S E   L E A __ L E T

B A N __ U E T   P A R __ N E R

A M A __ I N G   B A R __ A I N

U N S __ U N D   H A I __ N E T

C A R __ M E L   B R O __ L E R

K A T __ D I D   I R O __ I N G

B A N __ A N A   A N G __ I S H

P A C __ A G E   G L I __ T E N

T A D __ O L E   H I G __ W A Y

E A R __ O B E   G R A __ I T Y

C R U __ B L E   C O E __ I S T

Birthday Bloopers

There's something puzzling about this picture of Junior's birthday party. At least
eight mistakes have been made by the illustrator. How many can you find?

ANSWERS, PAGE 122

Jungle Survival

A Game for Two Players

GAME BY WAYNE SCHMITTBERGER / ILLUSTRATION BY PAUL RICHER

Setting Up

Copy or cut out the 20 pieces on the right. On the board above, arrange them so that their numbers and colors match the diagram on the next page. No more than one piece may be placed on a single square.

How to Play

One player uses the red pieces, and the other player uses the white pieces. In turn, each player moves one of his or her pieces in a straight line, either horizontally, vertically, or diagonally. The number of squares a piece may move depends on the number shown on it:

Pieces with a "1" can only move one square.
Pieces with a "2" can move 1 or 2 squares.
Pieces with a "3" can move 1, 2, or 3 squares.
Pieces with a "4" can move 1, 2, 3, or 4 squares.

Pieces may not jump over other pieces.

Crossing the River

Starting Position

The row of squares in the middle of the board is called "the river." Pieces may move onto or across river squares in the usual way. But a piece that begins its move across the river (on the opponent's side of the board) may move any number of squares in a straight line, regardless of the number on it. (It still may not jump over other pieces, though.) It loses this power if it moves back onto its own side of the river, or onto the river itself.

Making Captures

Only one piece at a time may occupy a single square. A piece may capture an opposing piece by landing on it. Captured pieces are removed from the board and are out of play.

A piece may not capture a piece of the same type (for example, a toucan may not capture a toucan). A piece may capture any other type of piece, regardless of whether it has a higher or lower number.

Winning

The object of the game is to capture all the opponent's pieces of any one type: either the lion, or both elephants, or all three chimpanzees, or all four toucans. In other words, a player who does not have at least one of each type of animal loses.

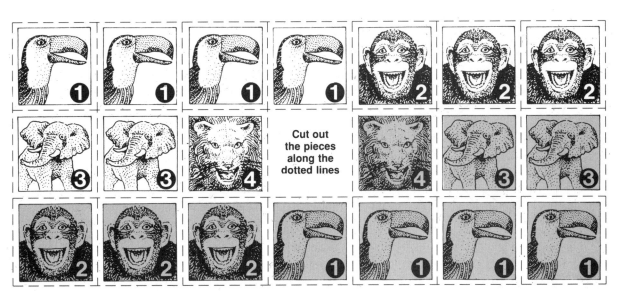

Cut out the pieces along the dotted lines

Triangle Tangle ❷

Color in each area that has exactly three sides, and you'll see
something that makes a big splash!

ANSWER, PAGE 122

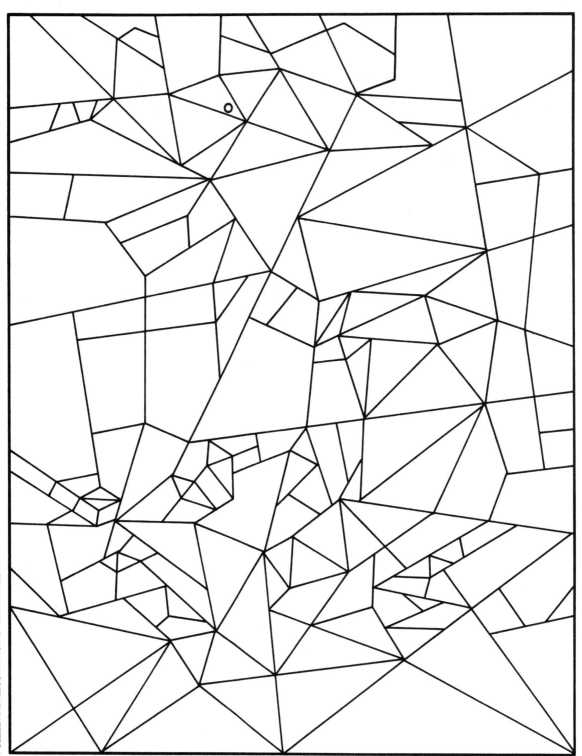

PUZZLE AND ILLUSTRATION BY MARK MAZUT

Crossword 3

ACROSS

1 Corn on the ___
4 Traffic ___ (highway problems)
8 Take a nap
12 Lemon or orange drink
13 Revise a manuscript
14 Where Adam and Eve lived
15 Man's formal neckwear
16 Bottom of a shoe
17 Require
18 Mails
20 Female sheep
22 Opposite of "no"
24 Bicycle speeds
28 Baseball great ___ Ruth
31 Eager
34 Garden tool
35 Employs
36 Small truck
37 Opposite of "yup"
38 Fib
39 Scream
40 Looks at
41 Loop of rope
43 So far
45 Leave, as a job
48 Positive trait
52 South American country
55 Cashews and almonds, for example
57 Tree-chopping tool
58 Region
59 Joint in the leg
60 Barbie's boyfriend
61 What Huck Finn sailed on
62 Animal that can balance a ball on its nose
63 Double curve in a road

DOWN

1 Dogs' enemies
2 Dog that Garfield likes to pick on
3 "I've ___ working on the railroad..."
4 Outlaw ___ James
5 Commotion
6 Track race distance, often
7 Meat and potatoes mixture
8 Closely packed
9 Type of poem
10 Name of the last letter in the alphabet
11 The ___ (finish of a movie)
19 Colors used for 21-Down on Easter
21 Thing colored with 19-Down on Easter
23 Put money in a piggy bank
25 Sailor's call
26 Noose material
27 Looks at
28 What a matador fights
29 The largest continent
30 Spelling contests
32 Young lady
33 Solitary
37 Tennis court dividers
39 "I am, ___ are, it is"
42 Sit Indian-style
44 Painter's stand
46 Fluids inside pens
47 Song
49 "For Pete's ___!"
50 Former spouses
51 Column between ones and hundreds
52 Good golfer's score
53 A long time
54 Football official, for short
56 Coffee alternative

PUZZLE BY PETER GORDON

Saurian Search

Seven tiny dinosaurs are hiding from the two big, hungry-looking dinosaurs in this scene. Can you spot them?

ANSWERS, PAGE 123

ILLUSTRATION BY PATRICIA WYNNE

Football Plays

The name of a football term is hidden in each sentence below. Each term reads from left to right and may be a part of more than one word. One example is underlined for you.

ANSWERS, PAGE 123

Ex: That dum**b lock**smith couldn't even get into his own house!

1. I loaned him the two bits, but I never did get my quarter back.
2. As he sat on the tack, we heard him shout, "Ouch! Down with jokers!"
3. Then he picked up the tack, left it on a table, and stormed off.
4. Please refer eerie events, occult occurrences, and strange things to me.
5. Do you feel safe tying knots in barbed wire?
6. He would skip assignments if his mother didn't check on him.
7. I didn't meet the chap until he stepped on my toe.
8. That was a superb owl you made in art class, Alyssa.
9. When they saw her fall off, side-saddle became less popular.
10. I didn't know that a boar is a pig's kin.

PUZZLE BY GEORGE BREDEHORN

The Middle Man

Fill the spaces in the center row with the last name of a former president of the United States to spell seven common three-letter words reading down.

ANSWER, PAGE 123

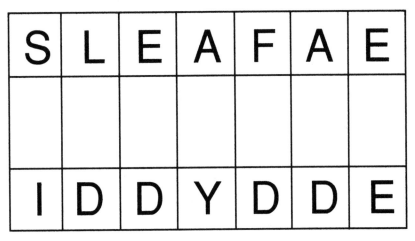

S	L	E	A	F	A	E
I	D	D	Y	D	D	E

PUZZLE BY ETHEL QUILLIN

Word **H**unt

Each of these people is thinking of a different word. The lengths of all the words are shown by the number of boxes. Can you figure out all the words?

ANSWERS, PAGE 122

My word rhymes with "chart." It's something I have in my hair.

ALAN

My word is something I'm holding. It's also something I do to my shoelaces.

BONNIE

Put the first three letters of Alan's word in front of Bonnie's word, add an "S" at the end, and you'll get fun events to go to on birthdays.

CURT

Break Irene's word into two parts between the double letters, put Alan's word in the middle, and you'll get a small place to store things.

DIANE

Rearrange the letters in my name to get a kind of grain.

ERIC

Change the "R" in Alan's word to an "N," and get something that hot dogs often do.

FRANK

Put Bonnie's word right in the middle of Frank's word, and you'll get someone a doctor takes care of.

GEORGI

Name the first punctuation mark you see in this sentence, and you will have my word.

HENRY

PUZZLE BY GEORGE BREDEHORN / ILLUSTRATIONS BY BARBARA STEADMAN

GAMES MAGAZINE PRESENTS

Riddle Search 3

The 19 fish listed below are hidden in the grid of letters. Look across, back, down, up, and diagonally in the letters, and circle each word you find. The word CARP has been circled as an example.

When you've correctly circled all 19 words, take the uncircled letters from the grid and write them on the blank spaces at the bottom of the page. Keep the letters in order, from left to right and from top to bottom, and you'll discover the answer to this riddle:

WHERE DO FISH SAVE THEIR MONEY?

ANSWER, PAGE 123

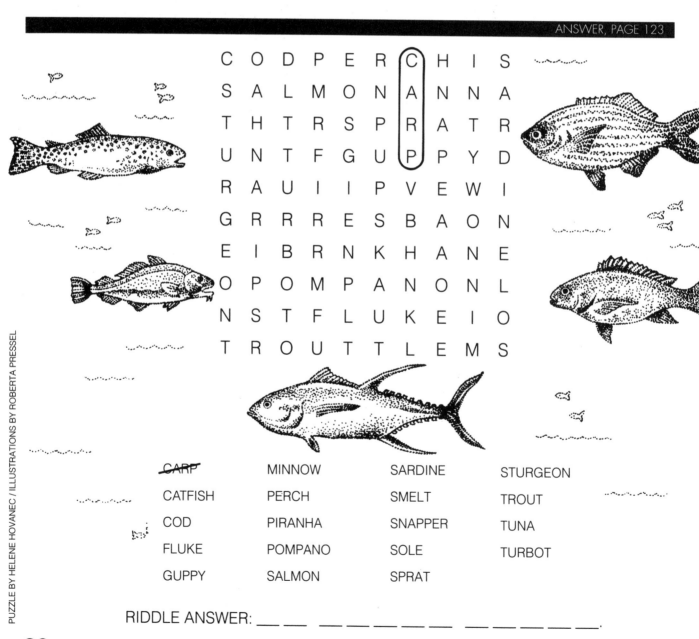

```
C  O  D  P  E  R  C  H  I  S
S  A  L  M  O  N  A  N  N  A
T  H  T  R  S  P  R  A  T  R
U  N  T  F  G  U  P  P  Y  D
R  A  U  I  I  P  V  E  W  I
G  R  R  R  E  S  B  A  O  N
E  I  B  R  N  K  H  A  N  E
O  P  O  M  P  A  N  O  N  L
N  S  T  F  L  U  K  E  I  O
T  R  O  U  T  T  L  E  M  S
```

CARP   MINNOW   SARDINE   STURGEON
CATFISH   PERCH   SMELT   TROUT
COD   PIRANHA   SNAPPER   TUNA
FLUKE   POMPANO   SOLE   TURBOT
GUPPY   SALMON   SPRAT

RIDDLE ANSWER: __ __ __ __ __ __ __ __ __ __ __ __ __ __.

Toying Around

How good is your memory? Study this playroom scene for up to two minutes.

Then turn the page for a quiz on what you've seen.

ILLUSTRATION BY TED ENIK

Toying Around

(PLEASE DON'T READ THIS UNTIL YOU HAVE READ THE PREVIOUS PAGE.)

A friend has borrowed three of the toys that were pictured on the preceding page. The toys shown below are still in the playroom. Can you determine (from memory) which toys are missing?

ANSWERS, PAGE 123

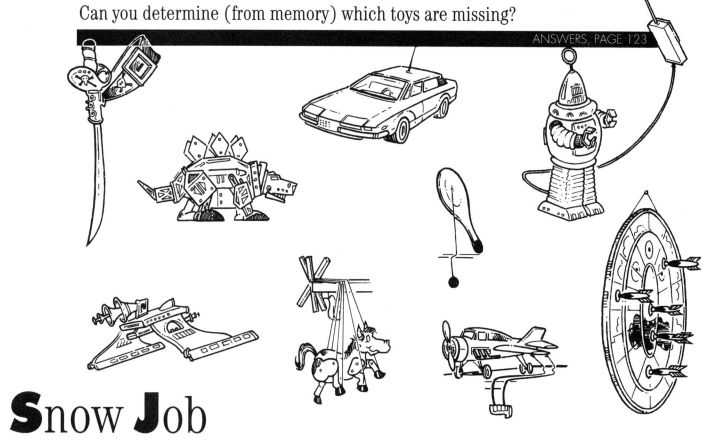

Snow Job

This snowman can't pull himself together. Can you match his left with his correct right half and make him whole again?

ANSWER, PAGE 123

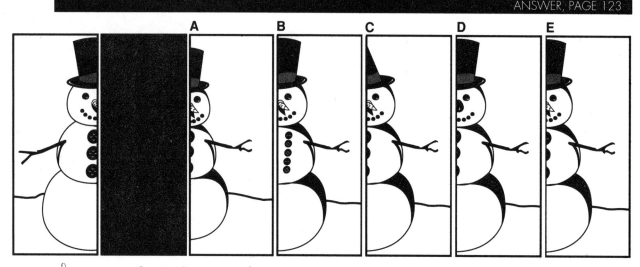

ILLUSTRATION BY HEIDI SCHMIDT

math into lesson on ruling thing out, eliminating wrong answers (study skills)

Connect the Dots Maze

This puzzle has two parts. First, connect the dots in order from 1 to 59 and your lines will form a maze. Then solve the maze by finding a path from START to END without crossing any lines.

ANSWER, PAGE 123

47•

46• 41•   •40

48•

                •49   22•   •23

        •50   27•   •26

51•

16•   •17

9•   •8   25•   •24

6•   •7   38•   •39

19•   •18   33•   •32

                                END

44•

•45

START

43•   •42

20•

                              •21

5•   4• 29•   •28

12•   •13   36•   •37

        35•   •34

        30•   •31

•3   •2

10• •11   •54   •55

15•   57•   •56

    •14

52•   •53 •58   59•   1•

Winter Wonder

Can you find 12 or more mistakes in this winter lodge scene?

ANSWERS, PAGE 123

PUZZLE BY KAREN ANDERSON / ILLUSTRATION BY LORETTA LUSTIG

Secret Recipes

Each of the nine nonsense lines below contains the names of two foods that go together. The letters in each word are in the correct order, but you need to unscramble the two parts.

ANSWERS, PAGE 123

Example: **PCAERAROST**S will give you **PEAS** and CARROTS.

1. S M P E A A T G B H A E L T T L I S
2. M C A H C E A E R O N I S E
3. L T E O T M T U A C T O E E S
4. B B R E U T A T D E R
5. H E A G G M S
6. R B E A I N C S E
7. M P O T A E T O A E T S
8. T D R U E R S K S I E N Y G
9. C D H U M I P C L I K N G E S N

Seeing Red

How many of these "red" words can you identify? Put one letter on each blank.

ANSWERS, PAGE 123

1. Boy's name   _ R E D
2. Make again   R E D _
3. Challenged   _ _ R E D
4. Employed   _ _ R E D
5. Cut in long narrow strips   _ _ R E D
6. Make less   R E D _ _ _
7. Rained heavily   _ _ _ R E D
8. Frightened   _ _ _ R E D
9. Forecast the future   _ R E D _ _ _
10. Giant evergreen tree   R E D _ _ _ _
11. Ready   _ _ _ _ _ R E D
12. Strolled around   _ _ _ _ _ R E D

Detective's **N**otebook **2**

FILE: CRIME SOLVING
CATEGORY: PICTURE MYSTERY

Sundays were usually slow at Police Headquarters. Officer Fred Dumpty was at his desk munching a donut and puzzling over the Sunday crossword. He was just about to fill in the answer to 6-Down ("Italian pie"—PIZZA, one of his favorite foods) when the phone rang. "Great," Dumpty grumbled. "Just when I was about to write my first answer in one of these things."

"Hello, police? This is Greg Winters," whispered a voice. "Quick, send someone to 28 Skyline Drive. There's someone in my bedroom. I can hear … "

The voice faded away. Dumpty could hear a sharp crack as the phone receiver hit something—probably the floor. Then he heard the muted voice of Mr. Winters shouting, "Hey, drop that! The police are on the way, they'll find you!"

Dumpty scrambled to his patrol car. Yes, he thought, as he drove toward Skyline Drive, the police are on the way. He enjoyed being a figure of law and order, and prided himself on his perfect crime-solving record.

When Dumpty arrived at the Winters' house, the front door was locked. At the rear of the house he found a concrete patio, and behind it a large wooded area. The back door was open. Preparing himself for the worst, Dumpty pulled out his revolver.

"I'm over here," shouted a voice behind him. Dumpty swung around and saw a man stumbling out of the woods. He was wearing a bathrobe and slippers. The slippers were covered with bits of wood and brambles.

"I'm Greg Winters," the man panted. "I'm afraid I lost him. He ran off toward the highway."

"Tell me what happened here,"

said Dumpty as he holstered his gun.

"I was reading in my den," said Winters, "when I heard funny noises. At first I thought It was kids playing in the street, but then I heard drawers opening and closing in my bedroom." Winters gestured toward the other end of the house. "That's when I called the police. Was it you I spoke to?"

Officer Dumpty nodded and glanced at the man's feet. Winters's slippers had rabbit faces on them. "What were you doing in the woods?" he asked.

"When I was on the phone with you," Winters explained, "I saw a man run into the woods. I dropped the phone and ran after him. I can usually run pretty fast, but these slippers held me back."

"Can you describe the man?" asked Dumpty.

"Well, he was wearing jeans and a gray sweatshirt, and he had

WRITTEN BY MARVIN MILLER / ILLUSTRATIONS BY PHIL SCHEUER

brown hair. But I only saw him from the back, I'm afraid it's not much help."

Dumpty looked at Greg's worried face. "We'd better go inside and see if anything is missing."

"I heard the guy go into my closet," said Greg. "I keep my coin collection in there. I hope he didn't steal it. It's worth a lot of money." He added, "At least I'm insured."

Dumpty took off his hat and scratched his head. "You know, Mr. Winters, I'll bet your coin collection *is* missing. But it wasn't stolen. I think you made up this story so that you could collect the insurance money."

BELOW LEFT IS A PICTURE OF OFFICER DUMPTY TALKING TO GREG WINTERS. WHY DID DUMPTY SUSPECT THAT THE ROBBERY WAS A FAKE?

FILE: SURVEILLANCE
CATEGORY: TOP SECRET

Sometimes a detective must watch a suspect without the person knowing he is being observed. You can pretend to be reading a magazine while still keeping your suspect under surveillance. Here's how:

Cut out a small circle from the front pages of an open magazine. Then, tape a small mirror on the opposite page.

Pretend to be reading the magazine. If your suspect is in front of you, watch him through the peephole. If he's behind you, hold the magazine so you can see him in the mirror.

FILE: MISCELLANEOUS
CATEGORY: MYSTERY RIDDLE

Officer Franklin responded to a police call. A woman was sitting on a 10th floor windowsill and threatening to jump. There were no awnings or ledges to break her fall to the concrete pavement below. As Franklin got out of his police car, she suddenly fell off the sill. But she wasn't hurt. WHAT HAPPENED?

FILE: CRIME INVESTIGATING
CATEGORY: QUESTIONING THE SUSPECT

Asking the right questions can help a detective solve a crime or catch a criminal. Here are three cases. After reading the facts, what *one* question would tell you whether or not the suspect was guilty?

#1   You board a train in search of a criminal, whom you suspect is on the train and heading for Greenville, 50 miles away. You believe he plans to flee the country from the Greenville airport. A man who looks like your suspect is reading a newspaper in the last car. The conductor tells you the man has no identification but claims to be going to Greenville for some shopping and plans to return that evening. WHAT DO YOU ASK THE SUSPECT?

#2   You trail a spy to a small farm village. You suspect he arrived that morning and is disguised as a farmer. You see a man who is hoeing a field and is dressed like a farmer. His dungarees are dirty. Beads of perspiration dot his forehead. He seems nervous as you approach him. WHAT DO YOU ASK HIM?

#3   You arrive at a mansion where there has been a burglary. The owner claims he found a window open and a valuable antique statue missing from the hallway. His dog Brutus sniffs the carpet where the statue once stood. The owner suspects his servant committed the robbery, but the burglar could have been a stranger. WHAT DO YOU ASK THE OWNER?

Magic **S**pots

Do you have eyes in the back of your head? Well, your friends will think so after you perform this trick!

Set some dominoes on a table, turn your back, and ask a friend to move a few of them. He'll be amazed when you face him again, turn over one of the dominoes, and tell him how many he moved! How will you know? The number of dots on the domino you turn over will tell you.

To make this trick work right, first be sure to arrange the dominoes as explained below. And also be sure that your friend moves the dominoes according to your instructions.

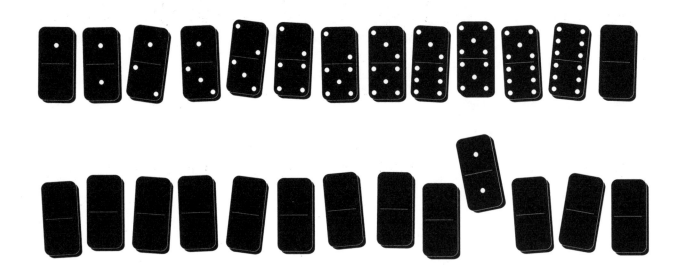

HOW THE TRICK IS DONE

Before your friend comes in, line up the dominoes as shown at top and turn them face down. Arrange them according to the number of dots they have, in increasing order from left to right.

When you've gotten them arranged face down, show them to your friend. Tell him that he may move up to 12 dominoes, but only one at a time, from the left end of the row to the right end of the row. Illustrate this by taking the first domino at the left (which you know has one dot) and putting it down at the right end. Then move the next domino (two dots) in the same way, and finally a third (three dots). Now you know that the domino on the left end of the row

has four dots. Remember that four—it's your key number!

Turn your back and ask your friend to move as many dominoes as he wants (but no more than 12). When he's finished, turn back to face him. Remembering your key number, turn over the fourth domino from the right end of the row (as shown in the second illustration). The number of dots on it will be the same as the number of dominoes your friend moved (two, here). If the domino is a blank, that means he tried to fool you by not moving any dominoes!

You can repeat this trick by looking at the domino that is now on the left and using its number of dots as your new key number.

WRITTEN BY MARVIN MILLER

D is for **D**ollhouse

How many things can you find in this dollhouse scene that begin with the letter D? If you're diligent, it shouldn't be too difficult to discover at least 30.

ANSWERS, PAGE 124

PUZZLE BY ANDREA CARLA MICHAELS / ILLUSTRATION BY BARBARA GRAY

Ice Patches

Can you slip the boxes at the bottom of the page into the correct spaces in the picture to complete the scene?

ANSWERS, PAGE 124

A

B

C

D

E

F

ILLUSTRATION BY DOUG JAMIESON

Crossword 4

ACROSS

1 House animal
4 Library item
8 Result of a knee scrape
12 "A long time ___" (much earlier)
13 "Me, myself, ___": 2 wds
14 Like a rooster or a stag
15 Brightly-colored bird that talks back
17 Angered
18 Admire lovingly
19 Got money for
21 Dry, like a desert
24 Bridal face coverings
27 Not right
30 Kentucky Derby or Indianapolis 500
32 Almond or cashew
33 Every single piece
34 What bats use to "see"
35 Pie ___ mode: 2 wds.
36 Abbreviation on American currency
37 "All's well that ___ well"
38 Wartime friend
39 Little devil
41 Shout
43 Involved with
45 Green spot in the desert
49 Ball-point writing tools
51 Small game bird
54 Egg on
55 Frog-like amphibian
56 Wedding words: 2 wds.
57 Horse pace
58 Divisions of a tennis match
59 Close to the ground

DOWN

1 Mama's husband
2 "Omigosh!"
3 Snowblower maker
4 Cake and cookie chef
5 Value of an ace in some games
6 Lyric poem
7 Sets of supplies, as for first aid
8 Grin from ear to ear
9 Bright red bird, or St. Louis team mascot
10 Ginger ___ (soft drink)
11 Area of planted roses
16 "I smell ___": 2 wds.
20 Done with
22 Tehran's country
23 Another name for 1-Down
25 Calm before a storm
26 Remain
27 Praise
28 Otherwise
29 Long-legged pink bird
31 Container for papers
34 Lease an apartment
38 "Oh, too bad!"
40 Beginning
42 Laundry bunches
44 Chooses
46 Ride a yacht
47 ___-Chinese (Southeast Asian)
48 Stash
49 Place
50 Make a boo-boo
52 Garden tool
53 Consume food

Say, Can You See?

There are 17 differences between the top and the bottom beach scene.

How many of the sea changes do you see?

ANSWERS, PAGE 124

ILLUSTRATIONS BY BOB ROSE

Spill the Beans

The names of the 13 kinds of beans listed below are hidden in the grid of letters. Look across, back, down, up, and diagonally in the letters, and circle each bean you discover. The word BAKED has been circled as an example.

When you've correctly circled all the beans, take the uncircled letters from the grid and write them on the blank spaces at the bottom of the page. Keep the letters in order, from left to right and from top to bottom, and you'll discover a phrase that means SPILL THE BEANS.

ANSWER, PAGE 124

BAKED   GREEN   LIMA   PINTO   SOY

BUTTER   KIDNEY   NAVY   SNAP   STRING

FRENCH   PEA   WAX

```
L  E  G  N  I  R  T  S
B  X  T  H  S  O  T  O
U  A  H  C  E  T  C  Y
T  W  K  N  P  N  A  V
T  T  O  E  G  I  U  A
E  T  A  R  D  P  A  N
R  O  E  F  F  M  T  H
Y  E  N  D  I  K  E  B
N  A  G  L  P  A  N  S
```

PHRASE: _ _ _ _ _ _ _ _ _ _ _ _ _ _ _ _ _ _ _ _ _ _.

One, Two, Three

Can you rank each of these sets of three items in order, according to the type of measurements given? Write a 1, 2, or 3 on each line to show your answers. For example, in the first set, place a 1 on the dash beside the structure that you think is tallest, a 2 on the dash beside the next tallest, and a 3 on the dash beside the shortest.

Figuring out these rankings is not as easy as "one, two, three," so take your best guesses when you have to. You'll find some facts and explanations in the . . .

ANSWERS, PAGE 124

1. MAN-MADE MONUMENTS (tallest to shortest)

____Eiffel Tower

____Great Pyramid of Cheops

____Washington Monument

2. CALORIES IN FRUIT (most to least per serving)

apple ____

peach ____

watermelon ____

3. COINS PRODUCED IN 1990 (most to least)

____pennies

____dimes

____quarters

4. ALL-TIME TOP TV PROGRAMS (most to least viewed)

Dallas ("Who shot J.R.?" episode) ____

M*A*S*H (final episode) ____

Superbowl XX (1986) ____

5. WEIGHTS OF REGULATION SPORTS BALLS (heaviest to lightest)

____basketball

____croquet ball

____volleyball

6. TOP RUNNING SPEED OF ANIMALS (fastest to slowest)

____ostrich

____pronghorn antelope

____red kangaroo

8. DISTANCE MEASURES (longest to shortest)

____one furlong

____one league

____one mile

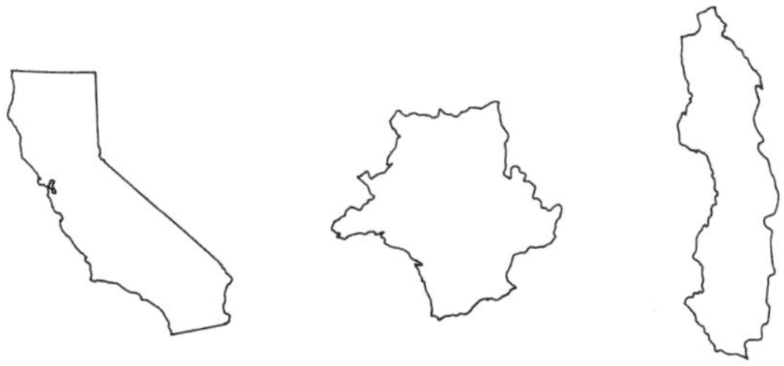

9. AREAS (largest to smallest)

California ____

France ____

Sweden ____

10. POPULATIONS OF WORLD CITIES (highest to lowest)

____Cairo, Egypt

____London, England

____Tokyo, Japan

Bonus: Where does New York City (the most populous U.S. city) fit into this ranking?

11. YEARS THAT STATES ENTERED THE UNION

(earliest to latest)

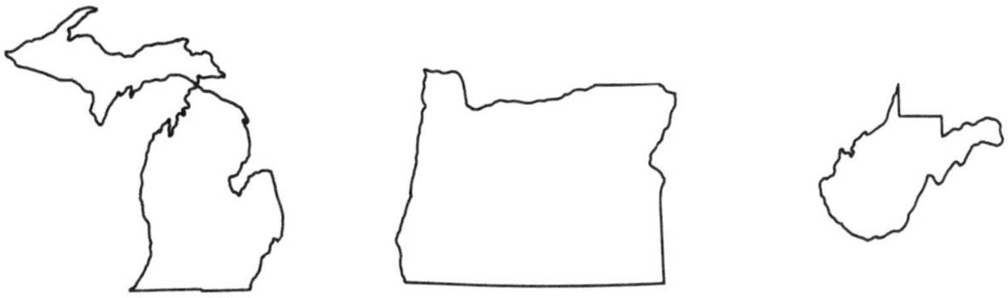

Michigan ____

Oregon ____

West Virginia ____

11. LENGTHS OF PLAYING AREAS (longest to shortest

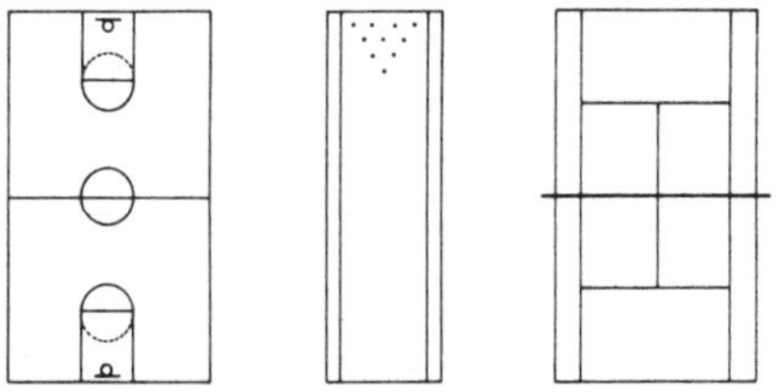

____basketball court

____bowling lane

____tennis court

Pie in the **S**ky

Each set of letters below is a scrambled name of a type of pie. If you unscramble each one and write the answers in the boxes, the answer to this riddle will read down the shaded column:

WHAT'S THE BEST THING TO PUT IN A PIE?

ANSWER, PAGE 124

PUZZLE BY HELENE HOVANEC

1. RHCEYR
2. ACCELHOOT
3. IKMNPPU
4. ACEMR
5. ACDRSTU
6. BBEELRRUY
7. ACENP
8. ALNTUW
9. FINHOCF

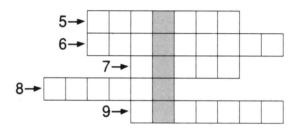

Word **W**eave

Solve the puzzle below like a miniature crossword puzzle—except that the answer to each clue will read both across and down. If you solve it correctly, you will form a five-letter word square.

ANSWER, PAGE 124

PUZZLE BY ETHEL QUILLIN

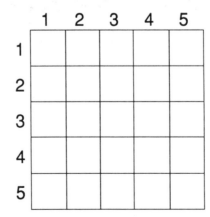

1 Long-necked bird or construction machine
2 Competitor
3 Stay away from
4 Simple-minded
5 Senior member of a tribe

Pencil Pointers 3

In this crossword puzzle, the clues appear inside the grid. Fill in the answers in the direction of the arrows.

Biblical song	__ Jose, Cal.	Plural of "is"	Zodiac lion	Be in charge of	Georgia or Texas	▼	By oneself	Crimson color	"__ la la"	Pigpen
▶	▼	▼	▼	▼	Small pies	▶	▼	▼	▼	▼
Place ▶					Watchful ▶					
Gas in some lights ▶					Not tomorrow / Males	▶				
Alter	The Cat in the __	Pie __ mode	Prayer word / Bite	▶		▼		Inquire	Golfing peg	Unhappy
▶	▼	▼				Has Dinner / Resort	▶	▼	▼	▼
E.T. and others ▶					▼	Ocean / Carmen, for one	▶			
Kind of dance ▶			Smart	Prodded / Clarinet part	▶					
TV dog	How old you are	Male off-spring	Cover a present / Turf	▶	▼			Raced	Hide __ seek	Cloud's place
▶	▼	▼	▼		Long periods of time	▶		▼	▼	▼
Long-necked bird ▶					__ and file	▶				
Stopped ▶					Raggedy Ann and __	▶				

Proverbial Confusion

Proverbs are supposed to offer good advice. But sometimes, different proverbs seem to say opposite things. We've taken three pairs of contradictory proverbs and mixed up the order of the words in each proverb. Can you unscramble them?

ANSWERS, PAGE 125

Pair #1

NEVER TOO TO LEARN IT'S LATE.
NEW DOG CAN'T TEACH AN OLD TRICKS YOU.

Pair #2

SHALL FIND AND SEEK YOU.
THE CAT KILLED CURIOSITY.

Pair #3

ONE TWO ARE BETTER THAN HEADS.
THE BROTH COOKS SPOIL TOO MANY.

Great Cats!

The names of seven large members of the cat family are hidden in the letter grid below. Each name is hidden in connecting squares. For example, TIGER can be spelled by starting at the T in the lower left corner, then moving up to the I, diagonally down to the G, diagonally up to the E, and down to the R. Can you find the other six great cats?

ANSWERS, PAGE 125

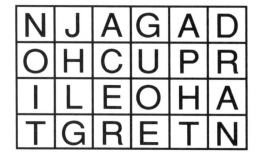

N	J	A	G	A	D
O	H	C	U	P	R
I	L	E	O	H	A
T	G	R	E	T	N

PUZZLE BY WAYNE SCHMITTBERGER

Puzzling Parade

Can you march through this picture and find 10 things wrong?

ANSWERS, PAGE 125

PUZZLE BY KAREN ANDERSON / ILLUSTRATION BY PHIL SCHEUER

Crisscross 3

Place the sewing words below into the diagram so that they interlock as in a crossword. Each of the words will be used exactly once, so you may cross them off as you use them. Try starting with the one nine-letter word—there is only one place it will fit.

ANSWER, PAGE 125

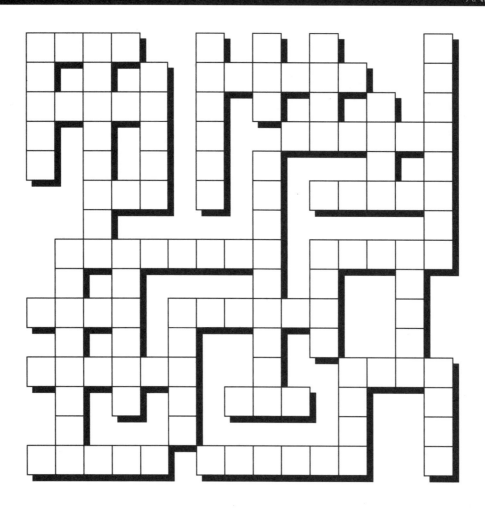

3 LETTERS	FELT	**5 LETTERS**	TULLE	BUTTON	CHAMBRAY
ARM	HEMP	CREPE	TWEED	EYELET	CRETONNE
SEW	LACE	DENIM		TASSEL	RESTITCH
TIE	LAMÉ	LISLE	**6 LETTERS**	VELVET	
	LAWN	MENDS	ALPACA		**9 LETTERS**
4 LETTERS	SILK	SERGE	ATTACH	**8 LETTERS**	POLYESTER
EDGE	TURN	SUEDE	BOUCLE	CASHMERE	

Out of **O**rder **4**

The panels of this comic strip are all mixed up. Can you unscramble the pictures so that they tell a story?

ANSWER, PAGE 125

A

B

C

D

E

F

PUZZLE AND ILLUSTRATION BY ROBERT LEIGHTON

Surround!

A Strategy Game for Two Players

To play Surround!, you need two pencils or pens of different colors (one for each player), and one of the game grids shown on these pages. After filling these grids, you can draw your own or use graph paper.

Rules

1. Players take turns coloring in any one space anywhere on the game grid. Each player uses a different color. (In the examples below, one player is using gray, and the other player is using red.) Neither player may pass (skip) his or her turn.

2. A player wins by "surrounding" either a **space** or a **connected group of spaces** of the opponent's color.

(i) A **space** is surrounded when it no longer borders at least one empty (uncolored) space (spaces touching only at corners don't count).

Examples:

The red space marked X is surrounded. Gray wins.

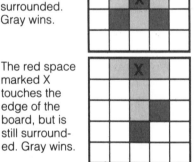

The red space marked X touches the edge of the board, but is still surrounded. Gray wins.

(ii) A **connected group of spaces** is surrounded when none of the spaces in the group touch at least one empty space.

Examples:
The gray group in the corner is not yet surrounded, since it touches the empty space marked X.

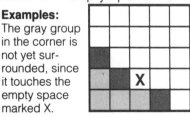

Red colors in the space marked X, surrounding the gray group. Red wins.

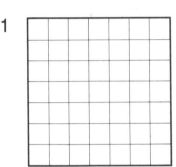

3. Sometimes a move will cause both players to have surrounded spaces or groups. If this happens, the player who made the move wins.

Examples:
In this position, the red group is not yet surrounded, since it touches the empty corner space marked X. But ...

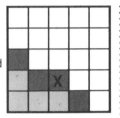

Gray colors in the corner space, surrounding the red group. Gray wins, even though the gray corner space is also surrounded.

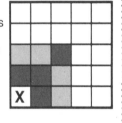

4. Finally, if a player makes a move that causes his or her own group to be surrounded, the player loses (unless the opponent is also surrounded, as in the last example).

Example:
It is Red's turn. No matter which empty space Red colors in, one of Red's own groups will become surrounded. Gray wins.

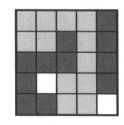

Game Grids

1

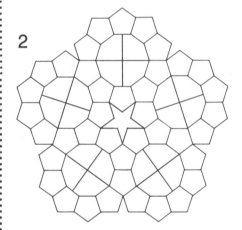

2

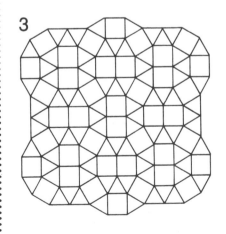

3

WRITTEN BY WAYNE SCHMITTBERGER

Strategy

Since the object of the game is to surround your opponent, you might think it's a good idea to start out by coloring in a space that touches one of your opponent's spaces. But if you do, you'll probably find out too late that you have only made it easier for your opponent to surround you!

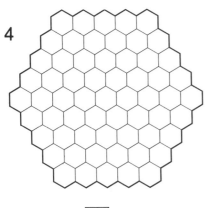

4

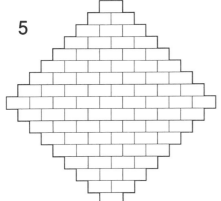

5

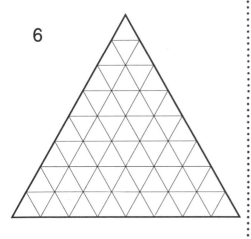

6

The best strategy, early in the game, is not to try to surround the opponent directly, but instead to try to surround groups of empty spaces. Here's why: When the game grid gets crowded, it will usually be safe for you to color in spaces within areas you control, but dangerous to color in spaces in areas your opponent controls. Whoever has surrounded more empty spaces, therefore, is likely to win.

In this position, for example, if either player colors in a space within the opponent's area, the opponent will be able to surround it in just one or two turns. Therefore, each player does best to color in spaces within their own areas. Since Gray has surrounded more empty spaces than Red, Gray is likely to win.

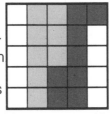

As the game continues, players might continue coloring spaces in the numerical order shown. As expected, Gray wins.

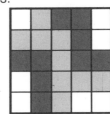

Things are not always this simple, though. A player who has surrounded more spaces than the opponent can sometimes lose, as the following diagram shows. Red has surrounded four spaces to Gray's three, but Gray will win, no matter whose turn it is. The reason is that Red, unlike Gray, has two separate groups, and must keep at least two empty spaces within each of them—which Red can no longer do. Once one of Red's groups is reduced to just one empty space, Gray will win by playing in that space.

And notice the position in this diagram. Gray has just played at X, inside an area that apparently had been Red's. Gray will now win because if Red plays at Y, Gray will play at Z (and vice versa). You'll discover many other tricky tactics as you play.

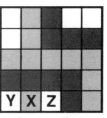

Playing on Different Game Grids

In the examples above, all the game grids were small and consisted of squares. But Surround! can be played on grids of any size and shape. We recommend using small grids for your first games. The larger the grid, the more complicated the play. Our favorite version is played on a grid of hexagons (like game grid number 4), but grids of squares, triangles, mixed shapes, and even irregular areas also lead to interesting play.

The Game of Go

Surround! is a new game, but it was inspired by the game of Go, which was invented in China between 2,000 and 4,000 years ago. Go is a board game that uses black and white pieces. Playing Go is similar to playing Surround! on a board of squares arranged in 19 rows and 19 columns, except that surrounding one space or group of spaces does not end the game. Instead, surrounded pieces are removed from the board, and play continues until both players pass. At the end, the player with the most "territory" (occupied spaces plus surrounded spaces) wins. To learn more about Go, check your local library or bookstore, or write for information to: American Go Association, P.O. Box 397, Old Chelsea Station, New York, NY 10113.

Categories

This puzzle is based on the old game of Categories. In each box, write the name of something that fits the category described at the left, and that also begins with the letter at the top. We've filled in an example to get you started.

ANSWERS, PAGE 125

PUZZLE BY KAREN ANDERSON

	S	M	A	R	T
Brands of chocolate-covered candy	SNICKERS				
Bodies of water					
Car makers					
One-word movie titles					
Hand-held tools					

Odd Cube Out

Each face of these four cubes is painted either black or white. If you could pick up each cube and look at all its faces, you would discover that three of the cubes are identical. You are told that cube B has four black faces, and that cube D does not have more than three black faces. Can you tell which cube is different from the others?

ANSWER, PAGE 125

PUZZLE BY GEORGE BREDEHORN

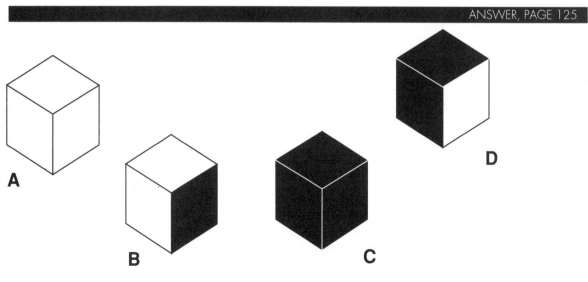

A

B

C

D

Creature Features

What two animals make up this creature's face?

ANSWERS, PAGE 125

PUZZLE BY PETER FAHRNI / PHOTOGRAPHS BY FRED WHITEHEAD AND JACK WILBURN

Winging **I**t

There are 26 birds well-hidden in the trees, plants, and sky in this scene. If you find 20,

you should feel as proud as a peacock. It will take an eagle eye to spot all 26 birds.

Eyeball Benders 3

By looking closely at the close-up pictures, can you identify the eight objects?

ANSWERS, PAGE 126

PHOTOGRAPHS BY KEITH GLASGOW

GAMES MAGAZINE PRESENTS

Rebus Ruckus

First, name each item pictured below. Then, add and subtract the letters in the names as indicated. If you do the puzzle correctly, the leftover letters will spell something that might involve leftovers.

ANSWER, PAGE 125

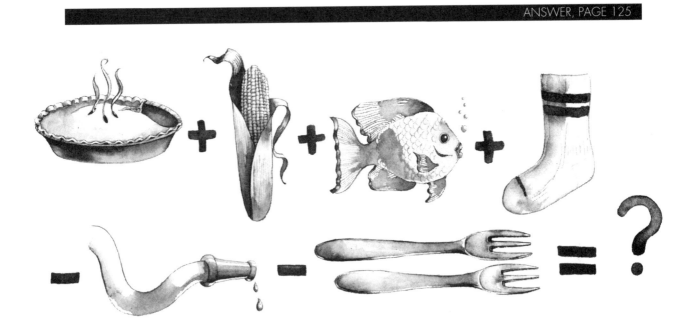

"Can" You Do It?

How many of these CAN words can you identify? Fill in each blank with one letter.

ANSWERS, PAGE 125

1. Walking stick — C A N _
2. Sweets — C A N _ _
3. Long, narrow boat — C A N _ _
4. Call off (an event) — C A N _ _ _
5. North American country — C A N _ _ _
6. Small yellow bird — C A N _ _ _
7. Dog-like — C A N _ _ _
8. Deep valley — C A N _ _ _
9. Campers' water holder — C A N _ _ _ _
10. Small container for flour — C A N _ _ _ _ _
11. Person running for office — C A N _ _ _ _ _ _
12. Orange-colored melon — C A N _ _ _ _ _ _ _

PUZZLE BY KAREN ANDERSON

Can **Y**ou **G**uess?

These tough trivia questions will stump nearly everyone. But see how many you can get right by making your best guess.

ANSWERS, PAGE 125

1. How many elephants are there in the United States?
____ 213
____ 692
____ 1,764
____ 12,198

2. About how many slices of pizza do Americans eat each year?
____ 500 million
____ 2 billion
____ 11 billion
____ 25 billion

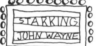

3. In how many movies did John Wayne play a leading role?
____ 23
____ 62
____ 113
____ 153
____ 15,000

4. We all know that movie stars receive enormous salaries nowadays for appearing in movies. In the 1931 film Frankenstein, how much did Boris Karloff get paid for portraying the monster?
____ $125 per week
____ $692 per week
____ $3,500 per week
____ $18,750 per week

5. To the closest 100,000, what was the population of the Los Angeles area according to the 1990 census?
____ 10,600,000
____ 12,600,000
____ 14,500,000
____ 16,500,000

6. How many video stores are there in the city of Bombay, India?
____ 15
____ 150
____ 1,500
____ 15,000

Paper Pinball

As in arcade pinball, your goal in this game is to score as many points as you can before exiting the board. Start at the topmost scorepost (worth 10 points) and travel along the paths, adding to (or subtracting from) your total score as you go. You may return to a scorepost you've used or cross over your path, but you may never retrace any part of your route. Because your score doesn't count until you get off the board, remember to leave a path clear to the exit. Use tracing paper (or write lightly) if you want to try the game more than once. A score of 240 or more points is excellent, 280 is superb, and 320 makes you a paper pinball pro! Our best score is 370 points.

ANSWER, PAGE 126

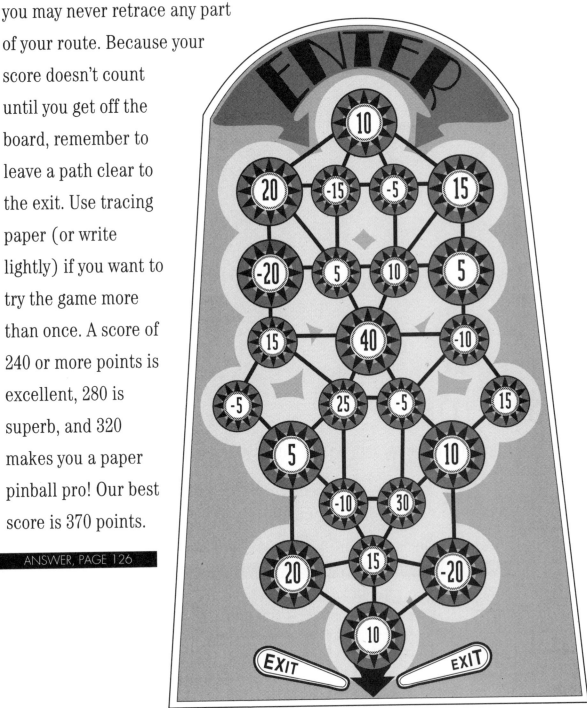

Match-Up 3

These six dolls may look alike at first glance. However, only two of them match exactly. Which two?

ANSWER, PAGE 125

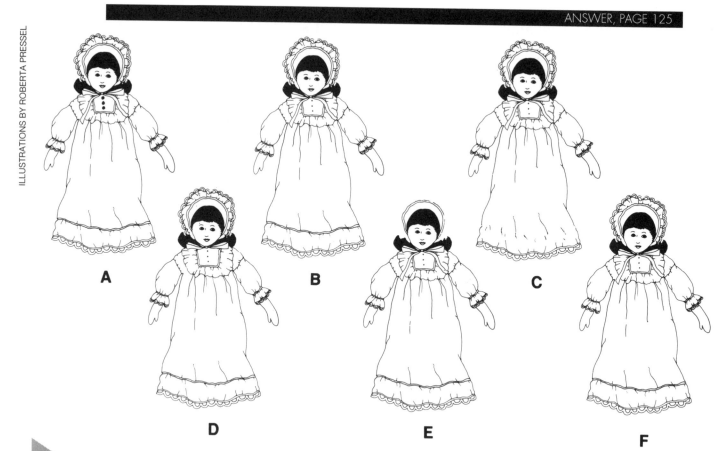

A   B   C

D   E   F

Cut-Ups

Each figure below can be cut into two identical pieces. As the example shows, the two pieces will have the same size and shape, even though they are turned in different directions. By cutting only along the thin lines, can you determine how to divide each figure into equal halves?

ANSWERS, PAGE 126

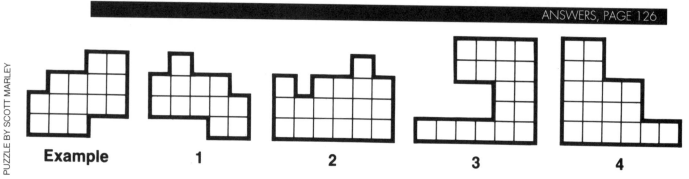

Example   1   2   3   4

ILLUSTRATIONS BY ROBERTA PRESSEL

PUZZLE BY SCOTT MARLEY

Scuba Search

These divers are so busy looking at the fish and underwater plants that they haven't noticed 15 familiar items hidden nearby. Can you find: a baby bottle, boot, comb, elephant, eyeglasses, football, glass with a stem, hat, mitten, pair of pants, pocket watch, stethoscope, toy sailboat, turtle, and wine bottle?

ANSWERS, PAGE 126

ILLUSTRATION BY VALA KONDO

Eyeball Benders 4

Can you identify the objects in these close-up photos, and figure out where you might find all of them?

ANSWERS, PAGE 126

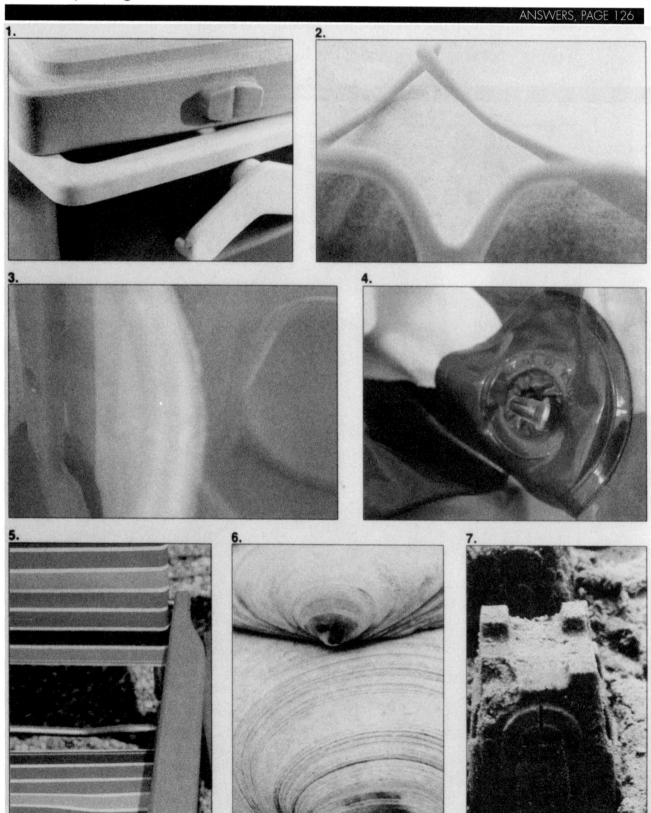

1.

2.

3.

4.

5.

6.

7.

Whose **H**ues?

To see a picture clearly, color the areas according to the letters:

Bl = blue, Br = brown, G = green, and R = red.

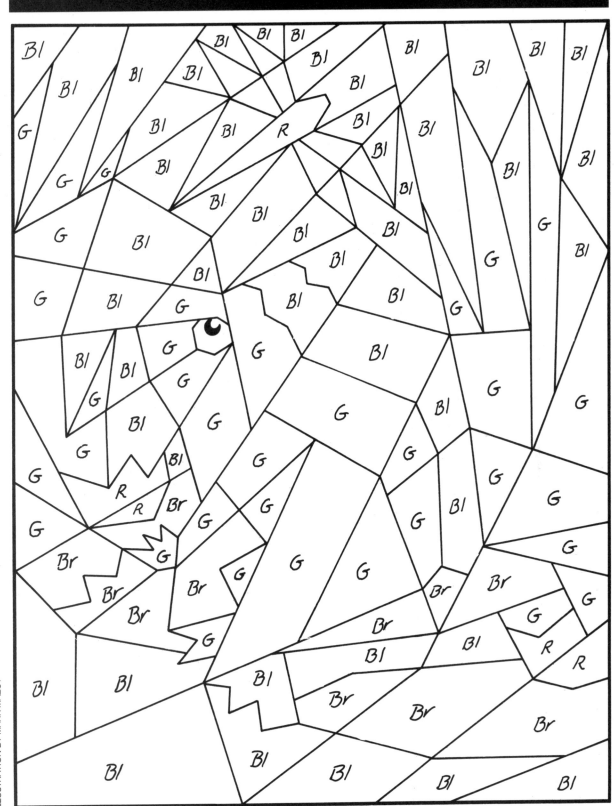

ILLUSTRATION BY MARK MAZUT

Answers

9 TRIANGLE TANGLE 1

10 EYEBALL BENDERS

1. Belt buckle
2. Pencil eraser tips
3. Starfish
4. Chewing gum
5. Life Savers candy
6. Sponge

11 PICTURE CROSSWORD 1

12 FILL-INS

13 BEAR MAZE

14 PENCIL POINTERS 1

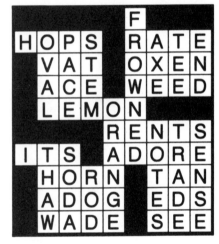

15 TARGET PRACTICE

Five arrows shot into the 15, 15, 7, 7, and 6 will total exactly 50 points.

20 CONNECT THE DOTS 1

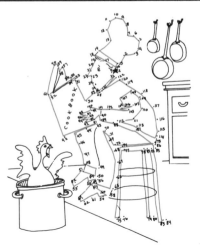

16 SHOE FITS

We found 13 errors:
1. A man is looking around the side of the closed store room door.
2. There is a mail slot on that door.
3. There is a women's shoe in the men's shoe display.
4. The percent symbol (%) is backward.
5. There's a boy reflected in the mirror who isn't in the room
6. One lace on the shoe by the door is too long.
7. The boy customer has a watch for a belt.
8. His sneaker has an electric cord attached.
9. The woman has two right feet.
10. The salesman has three hands.
11. The salesman's stool has a seat belt.
12. There is a shoe coming out of the side of the open box.
13. The loafer at the lower right has a tail.

17 RIDDLE SEARCH 1

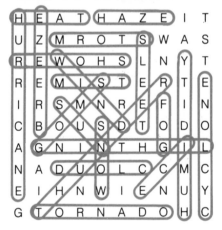

RIDDLE ANSWER: It wasn't raining.

18 MATCH-UP 1

Space shuttles A and E are alike.

19 OUT OF ORDER 1

The correct order is: D, B, E, A, F, C.

Cindy, age 7

Barbara, age 10

Eddy, age 5

Doug, age 7

Amy, age 6

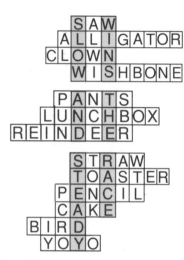

SAW
ALLIGATOR
CLOWN
WISHBONE

PANTS
LUNCHBOX
REINDEER

STRAW
TOASTER
PENCIL
CAKE
BIRD
YOYO

The leftover pictures: hare and tortoise. The phrase: Slow and steady wins the race.

24 TOUGH TEASERS

1. By plucking the goose
2. Sharon, Karen, and a third sister are triplets.
3. Because he only had two worms
4. None. Cats can't talk.
5. At the bottom
6. Because they had so many knights
7. To die of old age
8. "Men, get in the boat."

26 M IS FOR MALL

We found 53 items beginning with M in the picture. How about you?

Macaroni and cheese, magazines, magician, magnifying glass, mailbag, mailbox, mailman, majorette, make-up, mall, malt, manicurist, map, marbles, marine, marquee, Mars, masks, meadow (in mural), meat, megaphone, men, menu, mermaid, milk, mime, miniskirt, mink, mirror, mitt, mixer, mobile, moccasins, models (in toy store), Mohawk haircut (on Indian), monocle, money, monkey, monster, moon, moose, mop, moth, mother, mountain, mouse ears, mouth, mummy, mural, mushroom, music, mustache, mustard.

27 PICTURE THIS

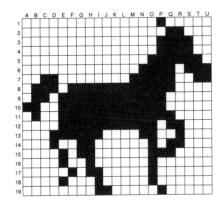

29 TRICKS AND TREATS

1. A wind-up mouse
2. A skeleton in a tuxedo
3. The mask
4. Gerry Moon
5. On the three
6. Ears of Indian corn
7. 1978
8. Five
9. Candy corn
10. Pumpkins A and C

30 CROSS MATH

9	÷	3	=	3
−		×		+
8	÷	2	=	4
=		=		=
1	+	6	=	7

36 LOST IN SPACE

28 CROSSWORD 1

J	A	R		T	H	I	S		S	T	A	R
A	R	E		H	I	D	E		H	A	T	E
W	E	E		O	P	E	N		A	G	E	D
S	A	F	E	S		A	D	A	M			
			D	E	W			D	E	S	K	S
S	M	O	G		A	U	L	D		H	I	T
W	A	V	E		G	S	A		C	O	L	E
A	L	E		B	E	A	M		H	E	L	P
P	E	N	N	Y			B	A	A			
			E	E	L	S		G	R	E	A	T
A	P	E	S		E	A	S	E		A	C	E
L	E	N	T		A	M	E	N		S	H	E
L	A	D	S		F	E	E	T		T	E	N

31 SUM FUN

PIZZA + SOAP + CAMEL − MAZE + ORANGE + SEVEN + M − LEAVES − MAGAZINES = POPCORN

34 COUNTRY PATHS

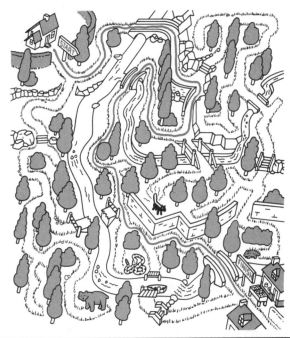

32 CONFUSABLES

1. A
2. A
3. B

The section fits into a U.S. map as shown:

4. penny B
   nickel A
   dime A
   quarter A
   dollar B

35 ROUND AND ROUND

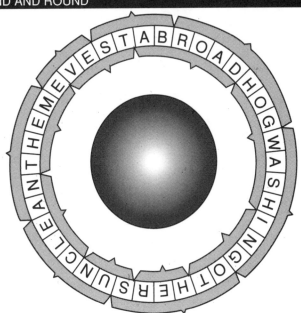

119

37 CRISSCROSS 1

```
M A R O O N   S A P P H I R E
A     R       C   L       R
G             A             O     C
E B O N Y   C R I M S O N       C A R
N             G   L       G     R E D
T     S E A G R E E N     R     D     I
A     I       B     I V O R Y   I     N
      L   V I O L E T     Y     H A Z E L
R E   U   E                     U     U
U   P E A C H     A M B E R     R     S
S     E       O           U     R
S E P I A     R           U     S
E           T A N   L     A   L A V E N D E R
```

38 PLAYING CARDS

We found 20 errors: 1) Man outside store disappears in window. 2) Kid's balloon comes inside store. 3) Tree is growing out of trash can. 4) Door with "push" sign opens wrong way. 5) Stuffed ducks have ears. 6) Frozen foods section. 7) Fire hydrant in store. 8) Christmas cards are in birthday section. 9) Man's shirt is on backward. 10) Heart-shaped boxes are labeled for St. Patrick's Day. 11) "Humorish" section 12) "Auto care" section. 13) "Get Sick" section. 14) Aces in St. Patrick's Day cards. 15) Woman is walking lizard. 16) Cash register faces out. 17) Digital clock reads 5:64. 18) Sign "Say I I love you with a card" has two I's. 19) Sign says to leave before paying. 20) Someone is shoplifting, and we all know that's wrong!

39 CROSSWORD 2

```
B I T   R A T   A N D S
A C E   E I O   T O R A H
D E E R F L Y   S T A L E
      T I S S U E   G E M
L A B E L   T A C O
E M U   E A S T   I N C H
N E T S   L I E   A F R O
A N T I   A P R S   L A P
    E X A M   T H Y M E
E R R   B O O B O O
D A F F Y   F I R E F L Y
S I L O S   I K E   R O E
  D Y E S   T E D   I T S
```

47 COMPUTER DATING

Julie should date Arthur, since that is the only choice that results in the three types of computers described:

#1 gave two incorrect statements

#2 gave two correct statements

#3 gave two correct statements (the first and third), and one incorrect statement (the middle one).

40 DETECTIVE'S NOTEBOOK 1

Picture Mystery

Nancy Gibson said she was looking through a magazine with the clubhouse door open. But the melted wax was on the front of the candle. If Nancy had been reading by candlelight, the breeze would have caused the dripped wax to spill down the other side of the candle—away from the door. Sherlock Holmes would have been proud of Dumpty.

Mystery Riddle

The policemen were facing each other.

Spotting Spots

A-2

B-6 (From higher up, the drop makes a harder splash.)

C-3

D-4

E-1

F-5 (This spot is running down the wall, while all the others are on the floor.)

42 INDIAN MAZE

44 UNDERSEA HUNT

46 PICTURE CROSSWORD 2

```
D A N D E L I O N   M O U T H
O       R   I   U       E     O
G   A   B E A R   R   B   S
H A N G E R     S   M O U S E
O   O   A M O E B A   B
U   N   R   R   R I B B O N
S F   P Y R A M I D L
E Y E     I   N   D   B E E S
    R   I   N   G G A   N
C A N O E   T E L E S C O P E
A   A   P         A   K   A
C   T   P   T O O T H P I C K
T R U M P E T     O   A   E
U   B   L   O       A C   R
S K A T E B O A R D   K E Y S
```

43 UNRHYMES

Other rhymes may be possible.

1. hour, four, tour
2. toes, does, shoes
3. soul, foul, ghoul
4. maid, said, plaid

43 SANTA SAYS ...

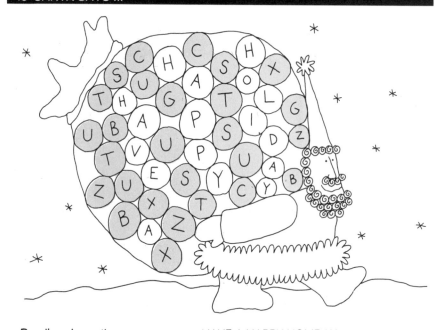

Reading down, the message says: HAVE A HAPPY HOLIDAY.

48 OUT OF ORDER 2

The correct order is: C, E, A, D, F, B.

49 FROM START TO FINISH

1-C   (sheep, wool sweater)
2-F   (maple tree, maple syrup)
3-A   (flower pollen, honey)
4-D   (coal, diamond)
5-E   (grapes, raisins)
6-B   (sand, glass)

50 PARTY MIX

The correct order is as follows:
1 - G (The table is ready for lunch, but no one has arrived yet.)
2 - C (Kids are arriving with presents.)
3 - H (Everyone is eating lunch.)
4 - D (Lunch is over, and the birthday girl is blowing out the candles on the cake.)
5 - B (Some kids are still eating cake, and others have finished. An unopened present can be seen.)
6 - E (Presents are being opened.)
7 - A (All the presents have been opened, and kids are playing a game.)
8 - F (Kids are leaving, taking party favors with them.)

52 RIDDLE SEARCH 2

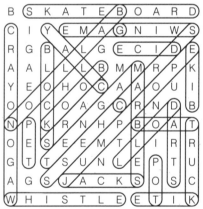

The answer to the riddle is: He was going BIG GAME HUNTING.

54 MATCH-UP 2

A and C are exactly alike.

53 SNOWBAWLING

1. He rolled him into a big snowball.
2. A cone from the construction on the street
3. No (two ornaments were still on the tree).
4. The scarf was checkered.
5. The flag was down.
6. One
7. No (there was a flock of birds).
8. There were six hats (three on the sledding hill, one on Junior, one on big brother, and one in the back of the car).
Bonus question: Garden Street (the name is on the mailbox).

55 WORD BINGO

The second (I) column down is the winner, using the words
WASTE/WAIST,
SCENTS/CENTS
PAIL/PALE,
GUESSED/GUEST,
SALE/SAIL.

57 B IS FOR BICYCLING

We found 60 items beginning with B in the picture. How about you?
Bag, baggage, baker (or bakery), ball (or baseball), balloons, bananas, bandage, bangs, banjo, banner, barrette, basket, bat, baton, bay, beads, beagle, beak, beanie, bear, beard, beaver, bee, beetle or bug (the Volkswagen), bell, belly, belt, bend (in the road), bicycle, bikini, billboard, binoculars, bird, blanket, blimp, block, blossom, board, boat, boathouse, body, bolt (of lightning), bone, book, boomerang, boot, bottle, boulder, bowl, boy, box, bread, brick, bridge, bucket, buckle, bus, bushes, butterfly, button.

61 SQUARED AWAY

F	A	C	T
I	S	L	E
L	E	A	N
L	A	N	D

O	R	A	L
P	A	R	E
E	V	E	N
N	E	A	T

61 BUILD A WORD

The new words are: ration, person, manage, kitten, forbid, father, donkey, carpet, candid, and button.

58 SHADY SHAPES

59 PICTURE CROSSWORD 3

60 EYEBALL BENDERS 2

The photos are close-ups of the following objects:

School bus	Blackboard eraser	Clock
Lockers		Looseleaf notebook
Paint-brushes	Milk carton	Basketball net and backboard

All of them can be found at a school.

62 OUT OF ORDER 3

The correct order is: C, F, D, B, E, A.

63 CONNECT THE DOTS 2

64 CRISSCROSS 2

```
S T O M A C H   M U S C L E S H
H       A     O     U     H   I
O   N A I L S   U   F     T O O T H
U     A     F     T O O T H   O
L I V E R         H   O       T H I G H
D   E       R     I     F   E   I
E   L U N G   R I F E     A B D O M E N   P
R   O     A B D O M E N   L       K
  C H E S T   C   R   L         K
T   E   E   F A C E   E         K
H E A D   A   G   H     E       I
R   R   K N E E   E Y E L I D   N
O   T   K       A   D   B       N
A     L E G   D   B O N E       Y
T O N G U E         W       Y
```

65 DRAGON MAZE

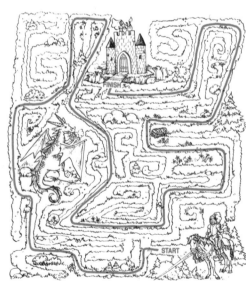

66 SKIN SWAP

1. C (fish, lion)
2. D (squirrel, zebra)
3. A (panda, parrot)
4. B (alligator, raccoon)

68 SCIENCE TEASERS

1. True.
2. False. The whip snaps because the very tip is going faster than the speed of sound. When it breaks the sound barrier, it produces the "crack."
3. True.
4. False. The currents created by the ice melting in the warm water will carry it to the edge of the bowl. The ice won't melt as quickly in the cold water, so it's more likely to stay in the center.

5. True.
6. True.
7. True.
8. False. The oil coats the mesh, but it is the surface tension (the "cling" between water molecules) that holds the water. Touching the bottom of the strainer will break the tension and allow the water to run through.
9. False. The slice of bread *may* land peanut butter side down, but if you drop it from higher up (say eight to ten feet), the bread will have enough time to make a full spin and may land with the peanut butter side up.
10. False. Rubber contracts when it is heated. Running the jar under hot water *will* help.

67 PENCIL POINTERS 2

70 ALPHABET STEW

In order, the 26 words are: Popcorn, chowder, disease, banquet, amazing, unsound, caramel, katydid, bandana, package, tadpole, earlobe, crumble, barbell, conjure, leaflet, partner, bargain, hairnet, broiler, ironing, anguish, glisten, highway, gravity, and coexist.

71 BIRTHDAY BLOOPERS

1. The Y in "BIRTHDAY" is hung upside down on the string.
2. On the cake, "birthday" is spelled "berthday."
3. The boy blowing out the candle has a shirt with a mismatched sleeve.
4. The flame of the candle is pointing toward the boy who is blowing on it.
5. A piece of cake has been cut, yet the cake is still whole.
6. The arm of the boy in the background should go behind the jar of apple juice, not in front of it. (You could also say that the boy's arm is too small compared to the jar.)
7. Steam is rising from the glass of cold apple juice.
8. The glass of juice is full, but so is the jar of juice.
9. Only five candles are visible at the top of the box, but there are at least seven candles inside it.

74 TRIANGLE TANGLE 2

75 CROSSWORD 3

```
C O B   J A M S   D O Z E
A D E   E D I T   E D E N
T I E   S O L E   N E E D
S E N D S   E W E S
        Y E S     G E A R S
B A B E   A G O G   H O E
U S E S   V A N   N O P E
L I E   Y E L L   E Y E S
L A S S O     Y E T
      Q U I T   A S S E T
P E R U   N U T S   A X E
A R E A   K N E E   K E N
R A F T   S E A L   E S S
```

78 WORD HUNT

Alan: PART
Bonnie: TIE
Curt: PARTIES
Diane: COMPART-MENT
Eric: RICE
Frank: PANT
Georgi: PATIENT
Henry: COMMA

Irene: COMMENT
John: ANT
Kate: STRAP
Larry: MASTER
Mary: PIRATE
Neil: CERTAIN
Olga: SURE
Peter: STREAM
Rita: TREASURE

76 SAURIAN SEARCH

77 FOOTBALL PLAYS

1. quarterback   6. pass
2. touchdown   7. punt
3. tackle   8. Superbowl
4. referee   9. off-sides
5. safety   10. pigskin

77 THE MIDDLE MAN

S	L	E	A	F	A	E
K	E	N	N	E	D	Y
I	D	D	Y	D	D	E

80 RIDDLE SEARCH 3

The answer to the riddle is: IN RIVER BANKS.

81 TOYING AROUND

The missing toys are the kite, the sailboat, and the Slinky.

82 SNOW JOB

Section E completes the snowman.

83 CONNECT THE DOTS MAZE

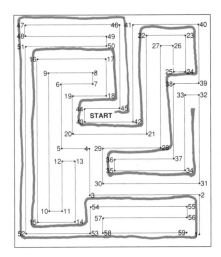

84 WINTER WONDER

We found 14 errors: 1) The fireplace tools include an oversized toothbrush. 2) The bear rug has two heads. 3) The chair back is a snow sled. 4) The couch has a dirrerent pattern on either side of the boy on it. 5) The boy on the couch is reading GAMES Junior upside down. 6) The counter's moulding disappears behind the stool. 7) The girl is raising a can of coffee to her lips. 8) An icicle is dripping through the closed window. 9) The hinges of the door and the handle are on the same side. 10) The "C" on the welcome mat is upside down. 11) One coat's sleeve is miscolored the color of the other. 12) An ice skate and a roller skate are paired up by the door. 13) The skis by the door are labeled K2 and 2K. 14) The cat has a pig's tail.

85 SECRET RECIPES

1. spaghetti and meatballs
2. macaroni and cheese
3. lettuce and tomatoes
4. bread and butter
5. ham and eggs
6. rice and beans
7. meat and potatoes
8. turkey and dressing
9. chicken and dumplings

85 SEEING RED

1. Fred; 2. redo; 3. dared; 4. hired; 5. shred; 6. reduce; 7. poured; 8. scared; 9. predict; 10. redwood; 11. prepared; 12. wandered

86 DETECTIVE'S NOTEBOOK 2

Picture Mystery

Through the window, Dumpty saw the receiver resting on the telephone cradle.

But he had heard the receiver fall to the floor as Winters supposedly ran after the thief. Caught by his mistake, Winters admitted setting up the robbery.

Mystery Riddle

The woman fell backward and landed inside the room.

Questioning the Suspect

1. WHERE IS YOUR TRAIN TICKET?

If the passenger were a fleeing criminal, he would have a one-way ticket.

2. MAY I SEE YOUR HANDS?

If the man's hands are not heavily calloused, chances are he's not a farmer.

3. DID THE DOG BARK?

If not, the robber must have been someone the dog knew—possibly the servant.

89 D IS FOR DOLLHOUSE

We found 37 things beginning with D in the picture. How about you?

Dachshund, dagger, daisies, dart, dartboard, December, deck (of cards), deer, desk, diamonds, diary, dice, dictionary, dimes, dinosaur, diploma, dish, divan, dog, doll, dollhouse, donkey, donuts, door, doorknob, doormat, dots, dragon, drapes, drawers, drawing, dress, drum, dryer, duck, dustmop, and dynamite.

90 ICE PATCHES

1. D
2. A
3. F
4. C
5. B
6. E

91 CROSSWORD 4

92 SAY, CAN YOU SEE?

The changes are indicated in red:

93 SPILL THE BEANS

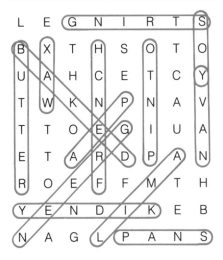

The answer to the riddle is: LETS THE CAT OUT OF THE BAG.

96 PIE IN THE SKY

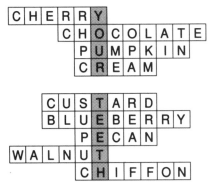

94 ONE, TWO, THREE

1. Eiffel Tower (985 feet), Washington Monument (555 ft.), Great Pyramid of Cheops (480 ft.)
2. watermelon (110 calories), apple (80), peach (40)
3. pennies (11,347,000,000), dimes (1,993,000,000), quarters (1,159,000,000)
4. *M*A*S*H,* Superbowl XX, *Dallas*
5. basketball (22.9 ounces), croquet ball (16.2 oz.), volleyball (9.88 oz.)
6. ostrich (50 miles per hour), red kangaroo (45 mph), pronghorn antelope (36 mph)
7. raven (69 years), alligator (55 yrs.), hippopotamus (40 yrs.)
8. one league (3 miles), one mile, one furlong (1/8 mile)
9. France, Sweden, California
10. Tokyo, London, Cairo. New York City has a smaller population than Tokyo, but is larger than London.
11. Michigan (1837), Oregon (1859), West Virginia (1863)
12. basketball court (85 feet), tennis court (78 ft.), bowling lane (60 ft.)

96 WORD WEAVE

C	R	A	N	E
R	I	V	A	L
A	V	O	I	D
N	A	I	V	E
E	L	D	E	R

97 PENCIL POINTERS 3

98 PROVERBIAL CONFUSION

Pair # 1
It's never too late to learn.
You can't teach an old dog new tricks.
Pair #2
Seek and you shall find.
Curiosity killed the cat.
Pair #3
Two heads are better than one.
Too many cooks spoil the broth.

98 GREAT CATS!

Besides TIGER, the cats hidden in the grid are CHEETAH, COUGAR, JAGUAR, LEOPARD, LION, and PANTHER.

99 PUZZLING PARADE

We found 10 errors: 1) On the American flag, the stars should be white on a colored background (and there should also be 50 stars). 2) The two street signs give different street names. 3) The yield sign says "STOP." 4) The hardware store is advertising a pasta special. 5) The drummer's drum is floating on air. 6) The "N" on "Town Hall" is backward. 7) The parade is supposed to start at noon, but it is 11:00. 8) One marcher is carrying an electric guitar. 9) There is an extra leg among the marchers. 10) There is a penguin in the street.

100 CRISSCROSS 3

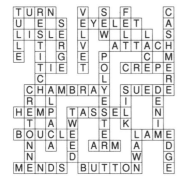

101 OUT OF ORDER 4

The correct order is: F, B, A, E, C, D.

104 CATEGORIES

Our answers are as follows. (Other answers are also possible):
Brands of chocolate-covered candy: Snickers, Mars, Almond Joy, Rolo, Twix; Bodies of water: (Lake) Superior, Mediterranean Sea, Atlantic Ocean, Red Sea, Thames River; Car makers: Saab, Mercedes, American Motors, Renault, Toyota; One-word movie titles: *Splash!, Mask, Alien, Rocky, Tootsie;* Hand-held tools: screwdriver, mallet, adz, rasp, trowel.

104 ODD CUBE OUT

Cube B is different from the others. Since B and D have different numbers of black faces, one of them must be the cube that is different. Since three white faces are visible on cube A, it cannot have more than three black faces, and therefore, it too must be different from B. Therefore, the cubes that match must be A, C, and D.

105 CREATURE FEATURES

An owl and a raccoon

106 WINGING IT

109 REBUS RUCKUS

PIE + CORN + FISH + SOCK - HOSE - FORKS = PICNIC

109 "CAN" YOU DO IT?

1. cane
2. candy
3. canoe
4. cancel
5. Canada
6. canary
7. canine
8. canyon
9. canteen
10. canister
11. candidate
12. cantaloupe

110 CAN YOU GUESS?

1. 692 (according to a survey done by the San Diego zoo)
2. 11 billion
3. 153 (more than any other Hollywood star)
4. $125 per week
5. 14,500,000
6. 15,000 (more than any other city in the world)

112 MATCH-UP 3

Dolls B and F are exactly alike.

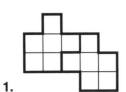
1.

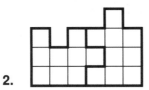
2.

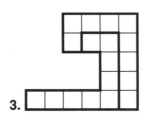
3.

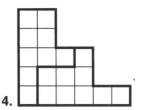
4.

108 EYEBALL BENDERS 3

1. typewriter
2. TV antennae
3. door stop
4. nail
5. coat hanger
6. bread bag and tie
7. sewing machine
8. camera film

114 EYEBALL BENDERS 4

1. Cooler
2. Sunglasses
3. Plastic shovel and pail
4. Beach ball
5. Beach chair
6. Clam shells
7. Sand castle

All of these objects can be found on the beach.

111 PAPER PINBALL

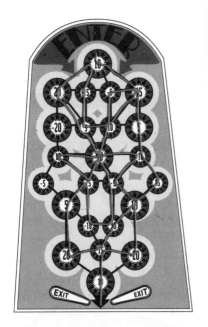

113 SCUBA SEARCH